Mike Cole skilfully utilizes the lens of public pedagogy to examine the increasingly hostile politics of the UK within this contemporary moment. By so doing, he shows the inextricable connection between conservative state policies and worsening conditions of racialization, violence, and economic decline, in lives of immigrant and other subaltern communities. In light of rising immigration and political antagonisms worldwide, Cole's book is indeed a timely contribution.

Antonia Darder, *Leavey Endowed Chair of Ethics & Moral Leadership,*
Loyola Marymount University, Los Angeles, USA

Theresa May's legacy will be the enduring images of 'Go Home' vans in neighbourhoods like mine, of children growing up without their parents and of black Britons being sent back to the Caribbean in chains. Not since Enoch Powell has Britain seen a minister so enthralled by the power of fear and hate.

Cole's book forensically examines May's time in office, the cost of which will be counted for years to come in the lost lives and livelihoods of those who have fought simply to live with dignity in an increasingly hostile environment.

Satbir Singh, *Chief Executive, The Joint Council for*
The Welfare of Immigrants (JCWI), UK

Through the theoretical lens of public pedagogy, Cole incisively takes apart Theresa May's hostile environment approach. This has been used to create misery for so many (including the author himself). The book is an exposé and the reader will be aghast at Cole's documentation of human-rights violations. The book crosses many disciplinary boundaries and will appeal to everyone interested in social justice and how to achieve it.

Alpesh Maisuria, *Senior Lecturer in Education Studies,*
University of East London, UK

Cole presents a Marxian discourse analysis of Theresa May in the form of an important case study of the interaction of media and policy that is urgently needed. This text investigates the cultural and economic scapegoating of the most vulnerable populations after the 2008 advent of the global recession, blame-placing simultaneously used by conservatives to enact and justify austerity measures. Far from being a 'moderate conservative' as is often portrayed via commentators, May has used her political position for years to cultivate racist and xenophobic policies that are linked with the global rise of the far right. The reader will be able to trace a direct line from May to the disaster that is Brexit, including making connections between immigration policy in the UK and other countries such as the US. Most importantly, the text serves as a blueprint for how conservative parties enable the far right in the hopes that they can achieve their political aims, along with how quickly they can then lose control of the narrative once that happens.

Faith Agostinone-Wilson, *Professor of Education,*
Aurora University, USA

Theresa May, The Hostile Environment and Public Pedagogies of Hate and Threat

Theresa May, The Hostile Environment and Public Pedagogies of Hate and Threat analyses Theresa May's involvement in the creation and promotion of public pedagogies of hate and threat around the issue of immigration, which are used to instil fear, stress and anxiety among large sections of the population.

This book uses public pedagogy as a theoretical lens and examines the economic and political backdrop to the hostile environment, before moving on to a consideration of its creation and consolidation by Theresa May as Home Secretary and later as Prime Minister. The effects of the hostile environment on health and education are addressed, as well as its specific impacts on asylum seekers and women. The book also interrogates the Windrush scandal and divided families, as well as the author and his family's personal experiences of the hostile environment. It concludes by considering the escalation of racism in general, the crisis in neoliberalism, and the case for a socialist future without borders.

This topical book will appeal to doctoral, postgraduate and advanced undergraduate students in the fields of education studies, pedagogy and sociology as well as those interested in UK politics.

Mike Cole is Professor in Education in The International Centre for Public Pedagogy, College of Professional Services at the University of East London, UK. He is the author of *Trump, the Alt-Right and Public Pedagogies of Hate and for Fascism: What Is To Be Done?* (Routledge, 2019).

Routledge Research in Education Policy and Politics

The Routledge Research in Education Policy and Politics series aims to enhance our understanding of key challenges and facilitate ongoing academic debate within the influential and growing field of Education Policy and Politics.

Books in the series include:

Academies and Free Schools in England
A History and Philosophy of The Gove Act
Adrian Hilton

Risk Society and School Educational Policy
Grant Rodwell

Neoliberalism and Market Forces in Education
Lessons from Sweden
Magnus Dahlstedt and Andreas Fejes

Reforming Principal Preparation at the State Level
Perspectives on Policy Reform from Illinois
Edited by Erika Hunt, Alicia Haller, Lisa Hood, and Maureen Kincaid

Theresa May, The Hostile Environment and Public Pedagogies of Hate and Threat
The Case for a Future Without Borders
Mike Cole

For more information about this series, please visit: www.routledge.com/ Routledge-Research-in-Education-Policy-and-Politics/book-series/RREPP

Theresa May, The Hostile Environment and Public Pedagogies of Hate and Threat

The Case for a Future Without Borders

Mike Cole

Routledge
Taylor & Francis Group

LONDON AND NEW YORK

First published 2020
by Routledge
2 Park Square, Milton Park, Abingdon, Oxon, OX14 4RN

and by Routledge
52 Vanderbilt Avenue, New York, NY 10017

Routledge is an imprint of the Taylor & Francis Group, an informa business

First issued in paperback 2021

British Library Cataloguing-in-Publication Data
A catalogue record for this book is available from the British Library

Library of Congress Cataloging-in-Publication Data
A catalog record has been requested for this book

ISBN: 978-0-367-22053-2 (hbk)
ISBN: 978-1-03-209155-6 (pbk)
ISBN: 978-0-429-27049-9 (ebk)

Typeset in Times New Roman
by Wearset Ltd, Boldon, Tyne and Wear

This book is dedicated to all those oppressed and exploited peoples who, against all odds and despite the trauma of attempting to enter hostile environments, bravely pursue the universal, fundamental and basic human right to live securely, freely, without violence, and with dignity

Contents

Acknowledgements

I would like to thank Lyka Cole, Alpesh Maisuria, Glenn Rikowski and Malise Rosbech for their help in writing this book. Special thanks to our immigration solicitor Paul Ward of James and Co for all his efforts in navigating us through the hostile environment. Their inclusion here does not necessarily imply agreement with all of the content of the book and, of course, any inadequacies in the analysis remain mine.

Introduction

When a country uses draconian terror legislation against people for peaceful protest, snatches others from their homes in dawn raids, incarcerates them without time limit and forces them onto planes in the middle of the night, due to take them to places where their lives might be at risk, something is very seriously wrong.

(The 'Stansted 15', on receiving suspended jail terms and community orders for attempting to stop an immigration deportation flight at Stansted Airport in March 2017, having been accused under terror legislation of endangering the safety of an airport, cited in Electronic Immigration Network [EIN], 7 February 2019)

This book is about the creation of, and promotion by, Theresa May of the 'really hostile environment', initiated in an interview with May in the *Telegraph* on 25 May 2012. In the book, I use public pedagogy (education that takes place outside traditional educational institutions and elaborated upon in the next section of this Introduction) as a theoretical lens through which to view this ruthless project, enacted under her stewardship, first as Home Secretary and then as Prime Minister. The hostile environment entails public pedagogies of hate and threat around the issue of immigration that is used to instil fear, stress and anxiety among large sections of the population. The pedagogies are accompanied by aggressive policies and highly restrictive immigration legislation.[1]

I examine both the development of the hostile environment per se, and how it has affected, and continues to affect, individuals and families. The intended effects, it is argued, are personal hardship and financial struggle, as part of an assault on individuals and family life that leads to division and turmoil, and that undermines human rights for (prospective) migrants and for families. May's overall intention is to deter immigrants from entering the UK and is part of her long-term and ongoing obsession with reducing net migration to the tens of thousands, rather than hundreds of thousands.

As well as immigrants, the promotion of the hostile environment serves to root out people already here, perceived to be 'illegal', or not able to (easily) prove 'legality', and targets long-term British citizens who have been in the UK for many decades who are not able to verify their citizenship.

The hostile environment scapegoats vulnerable people and blames them for the dire consequences of Conservative (Tory) austerity measures, and in addition to being one of Theresa May's key driving forces, appeases the Tory hard right, such as the European Research Group (ERG) and those racists who vote for the Conservatives, and works to contain the (future) rise of UKIP, and/or any other subsequent right to far right populist party or parties.

Public pedagogy

In this book I use public pedagogy as a theoretical lens through which to analyse discourse.

What is public pedagogy?

Social justice educator Roger Simon (1995, 109) has argued that pedagogy as a concept lends itself to a variety of sites for education to take place, that are 'multiple, shifting and overlapping'. The concept of *public* pedagogy has been defined by key public pedagogy theorists Jennifer Sandlin, Michael O'Malley and Jake Burdick as 'educational activity and learning in extrainstitutional spaces and discourses' (Sandlin *et al.*, 2011, 338).[2] Public pedagogy, they go on,

> has been largely constructed as a concept focusing on various forms, processes, and sites of education and learning occurring beyond formal schooling and is distinct from hidden and explicit curricula operating within and through school sites.[3]
>
> (Sandlin *et al.*, 2011, 338–339)

'Public pedagogy' has appeared in academic literature since 1894, but its presence has only been significant since the end of the twentieth century, having greatly increased since 2006 (Sandlin *et al.*, 2011, figure 1, p. 341). One of its foremost advocates, Henry Giroux, commends the work of David Trend (1992), Roger Simon (e.g. 1992, 1995) and others for extending pedagogy's 'application far beyond the classroom while also attempting to combine the cultural and the pedagogical as part of a broader vision of political education and cultural studies' (Giroux, 2004, 61). As Sandlin *et al.* (2011) explain, public pedagogy involves learning in educational sites such as popular culture, media, commercial spaces and the Internet; and through figures and sites of activism, including public intellectuals and grass-roots social movements. In addition, Donna Kerr (1999) locates pedagogy within the act of public speech itself. Public pedagogy scholars thus pose a multidimensional understanding of public education in democratic societies and relate it to 'the development of the ideological social-political nation within the consciousness and lived practices of that nation's citizenry' (Sandlin *et al.*, 2011, 342).[4]

Promoting progressive social change

The overwhelming focus of the majority of historical and contemporary public pedagogy theorists has been on the promotion of social justice for all. To this end, as Sandlin *et al.* (2011) point out, many have been involved in a counter-hegemonic project against neoliberal capitalism and its multiple manifestations per se, and/or against the oppression of multiple identities, such as gender, 'race',[5] age, sexual orientation, and social class that it upholds. Moreover, although

> the context and meaning of [public pedagogy] differ[s] in early sources from current parlance, in some ways the general axiological import remains consistent – the term in its earliest usage [dating back to 1894] implied a form of educational discourse in the service of the *public good*.
> (Sandlin *et al.*, 2011, 341–342)

A central contribution to public pedagogy has been from feminist scholars, who have argued that the teaching and learning inherent in everyday life can be both oppressive and resistant.
> (Luke, 1994, 1996; Sandlin *et al.*, 2011, 344)

Promoting hate and fascism

Public pedagogy analysis has also been deployed to look at ways in which oppressive discourses are permeated. Thus Giroux (2010, 7) refers to a 'public pedagogy of hate' in the US, emitted by a 'right-wing spin machine', influenced by the right-wing media, in particular conservative radio talk show hosts, that 'endlessly spews out a toxic rhetoric' against Muslims, African Americans and other people of colour, immigrants, and many other groups (Giroux, 2010, 8).

In a recent book (Cole, 2019, chapters 2, 3 and 4; see also Cole, forthcoming), I developed and extended Giroux's public pedagogy of hate to understand how Donald J. Trump promotes hatred through his speeches and via Twitter. Trump's public pedagogy of hate serves not only as an attempt to 'educate' the public at large, often to promote racism, sexism and climate change misinformation, and, on one occasion, to mock disability, but also to embolden and legitimize the views of individuals and groups associated with the alternative right or alt-right, and other far right groups with core fascist beliefs. Ongoing policies, I demonstrated, accompany Trump's public pedagogy. The alt-right, I argued, are also clearly and manifestly engaged in public pedagogies of hate, but also actively promoting a public pedagogy for fascism, both in their quest for a white supremacy and a white ethno-state and in terms of policy recommendations for a neo-Nazi USA that embodies some key elements of classic fascism. The genesis and development of that book resonated with Sandlin *et al.*'s (2011, 363) call for 'increased efforts by researchers, activists, artists, and practitioners to take up questions around educations that exist outside of institutional purview', stressing the need to address 'the species of pedagogy occurring in public spaces that might still elude our vision' (Sandlin *et al.*, 2011, 364). The public pedagogies of Trump and the alt-right are two such public spaces that had previously not been comprehensively analysed within public pedagogy literature. Just as Giroux (1998, 2000), in Sandlin *et al.*'s (2011, 344) words, is 'collectively subverting dominant ideologies', so are Trump and the alt-right, but from the perspective of the radical right rather than from the left. Whereas, as noted, public pedagogy has traditionally been for *more* social justice and more equality, that of Trump and the alt-right, I argued in Cole, 2019, is from the viewpoint of progressives, for *less* justice and equality. Thus Trump and the alt-right can be viewed as attempting to subvert 'liberal democracy' (e.g. Shattuck *et al.*, 2018).

In Cole (2019), I also introduced new public pedagogies, including anti-fascist (pp. 94–95), anti-capitalist and pro-socialist pedagogies (pp. 97–115), which go beyond the social justice agenda of progressive public pedagogy theory, as well as a 'public pedagogy for ecology'; a 'public pedagogy of love' and a 'public pedagogy in reverse', this last formulation referring to Trump's use of 'fake news' to discredit anything that he feels undermines him, as far as certain news outlets are concerned: 'don't take any notice of them because you are being misinformed'. In this book, which focuses on Theresa May, I extend public pedagogy formulations still further, and thus further address Sandlin *et al.*'s (2011, 363) plea for greater elucidation of the efficacy of public pedagogy in illuminating unexamined pedagogy outside of formal educational institutions, specifically to further explore anti-progressive public pedagogies of hostility as well as of hate, thus continuing to engage in Sandlin *et al.*'s (2011, 363–364) call for more work by researchers to take up educations that occur outside institutions that are not generally perceived to be 'educational'. Importantly, I develop new articulations of socialist public pedagogy, including the inevitability and socially just imperative of open borders.

From Trump to May

While Trumpism has led to an increase in hatred *in general*, what Trump and May share in common is that they have both massively upped the barometer of racism, as well as unsurprisingly both being scored 'somewhat populist' in a major study (Lewis *et al.*, 2019).

The theoretical orientation of this book is Marxist. I take the position that it is a Marxist analysis that best explains the ascendancy of Theresa May (see the first section of Chapter 1, where I discuss the economic and political backdrop to the hostile environment[6]), and that also best informs a future socialist politics in a world without borders (see Chapter 5). However, it is not only those on the Left who have noted the ideological affinity between Trump and May. In his address to the UK Liberal Democrat Party's conference in March 2017, its then leader, Tim Farron summarized some key political similarities between Trump and May. Farron referred to the 'indecent haste with which Theresa May dashed to Washington DC to meet President Trump [...] less than a week after Donald Trump became president', the first world leader to do so: 'It wasn't just that ... [the urgent liaison] looked desperate – begging for a new deal as we cut our ties with Europe. It was because', he continued, 'of the world view that Donald Trump represents' (cited in Lindsay, 2017). As Farron argued:

> Here is a man who is building a wall, banning Muslims, telling the world that climate change is a conspiracy. A man who ridicules people with disabilities and jokes about sexually assaulting women. A man who claimed that President Obama wasn't born in the USA. [...] And it sent a very clear message. Britain is leaving behind our neighbours in Europe and all they stand for and hitching ourselves to Donald Trump and all he stands for is the new normal, the new status quo. Aggressive. Nationalistic.
>
> (Cited in Lindsay, 2017)

During her infamous meeting with Trump, May mouthed enthusiasm for his election result – 'stunning', and what it meant for 'blood relationships' – 'kinship':

Thank you for inviting me so soon after your inauguration and I'm delighted to be able to congratulate you on what was a *stunning* election victory. And, as you say, the invitation is an indication of the strength and importance of the special relationship that exists between our two countries, a relationship based on the bonds of history, of family, *kinship* and common interests.

(Cited in Campbell, 2017; emphasis added)

May then told of an unprecedented visit:

And in a further sign of the importance of that relationship I have today been able to convey Her Majesty the Queen's hope that President Trump and the First Lady would pay a state visit to the United Kingdom later this year and I'm delighted that the president has accepted that invitation.[7]

(Cited in Campbell, 2017)

May's dallying with Trump puts her, according to Farron 'to the right of Thatcher' (cited in Lindsay, 2017). Given Conservative Prime Minister Margaret Thatcher's enthusiasm for the ruthless Chilean military dictator Augusto Pinochet (Cole, 2018c, 276, 296, note 8), it is quite likely that Thatcher would also have fawned to Trump had history been different.[8]

While Farron has a good track record of opposition to racism, this intervention was in effect and in intent an open and over-optimistic bid to replace the Labour Party as the main party of opposition. It is littered with references to how progressive his Liberal Democratic Party is, but in fact the party is solidly pro-capitalist and, as we shall see in Chapter 1, formed a coalition government with the Conservatives for a period of five years. Moreover, rather than the internationalist outlook that would have informed a progressive speech, Farron's address was centred around patriotism – 'the most emotive and unifying thing that we have as a society' – and the [patently false] notion that 'the old debate between left and right, capitalism versus socialism' is over (cited in Lindsay, 2017).

Outline of the book

In the first chapter of the book, I begin by addressing the economic and political backdrop to the 'really hostile environment', initiated by Theresa May, then Home Secretary in May 2012. Its genesis needs to be seen in the light of the financial crash of 2007–2008 and the onset of the Great Recession, followed by the austerity measures implemented first by a Tory-led coalition, and then by the Conservative Party itself. In order to make sense of the relationship between austerity and the hostile environment, forged in a blanket public pedagogy of hate around the issue of immigration, and the deployment by the Tories of 'the "race" card' in the lead-up to the 2010 General Election (that resulted in the ConDem coalition Government), I introduce the Marxist concept of racialization. Having set this toxic background, I move on to an analysis of the naming, creation and consolidation by May of the hostile environment itself. This entailed the fostering of a most reactionary climate of fear directed at some of the UK's most vulnerable people. The hostile environment is accompanied by draconian policies, regulations, legislation and rules, centred around May's ideological and political obsession with reducing net annual migration to below one-hundred-thousand, and to be the one to herald the permanent cessation of free movement of workers. I focus in this chapter on May's stewardship of the Home Office. In so doing, I note key changes in family migration rules, May's controversial 'go home vans' and her moving of the second reading of the Immigration Bill in 2013. The subsequent 2014 Act is viewed in the context of ongoing racism in the run-up to the 2015 General Election, a racism that I demonstrate was not confined to the Tory Party. The result of the election was an outright majority for the Tories under Cameron.

In Chapter 2, I begin by noting that, on winning the 2015 General Election, David Cameron named Theresa May as a possible successor. I move on to an analysis of May's 2015 speech to the Conservative Party Conference, in essence a bid for Conservative Party leadership. In the speech, consistent with her established ideological orientation, May uses public pedagogies of hate and threat, in an attempt to win over the Tory faithful, and to scupper UKIP. I go on to address the 2016 Immigration Act that amounted to a 'doubling up' on 'hostile environment' policies. Following the pro-Europe Cameron's resignation in the light of a 'leave' victory in the EU referendum, May's ambition came to fruition and she became Prime Minister. I continue the chapter, therefore, with a consideration of her fragile and unstable premiership. I discuss her offensive against international students, and her relationship with Donald Trump and his world view, which has been critiqued by leading Liberal Democrat, Tim Farron. I go on to address the 8 June 2017 snap General Election, a disastrous and failed attempt to crush all opposition to her. Next, I consider May's pledge to end free movement once and for all, and her 'jump the queue' remark concerning EU nationals. I conclude the chapter with an evaluation of the 2018 White Paper on Immigration that has been described as the biggest single attack on migrant rights in a generation.

I begin Chapter 3 of the book with some snapshots of the 'really hostile environment' in action – in health and education. I go on to consider its overall impact on asylum seekers with respect to accommodation, the right to work, and detention. I then address the effect of the hostile environment on asylum seekers who are victims of torture, before looking at the issues surrounding migrants trying to cross the English Channel, and Home Secretary, Sajid Javid's response to this. I end the section on asylum seekers with a consideration of health care, and what happens if refugee status is granted. I conclude the chapter with an analysis of the specific impact of the 'really hostile environment' on women, with respect to both detention and domestic violence. As concerns the latter, I include a critical analysis of the Domestic Violence and Abuse Bill.

In Chapter 4, I begin by looking at an extraordinary event that became known as the Windrush scandal and that came to light in 2018. British subjects, mainly from the Caribbean, who had arrived in the UK before 1973, were detained, denied legal rights, threatened with deportation and some actually wrongly deported. I then consider families more generally who were, or are, divided directly as a result of the effects of the hostile environment, and examine what it actually costs in financial terms to obtain various UK visas, and ultimately for those who want it, UK citizenship. At the end of the chapter, I provide a personal testimony which outlines my own family's and my direct encounter with the hostile environment and of being in a divided family, and estimate the costs for us, both in financial and emotional terms.

In the final chapter, I begin by posing the question, is the hostile environment crumbling or being ramped up? I move on to a discussion of what many see as a crisis on neoliberalism, a crisis that is receptive and potentially conducive to the promotion of public pedagogies for socialism. Accordingly, I then make the case for what I consider to be the urgent need for a left-led Labour Government. In so doing, I outline what such a government might look like before concluding by briefly making the case for a socialist future without borders.

Notes

1 For ongoing updates to UK immigration legislation, see GOV.UK (Ongoing).
2 This first section of this Introduction on public pedagogy draws on Cole (2019, 2–4).
3 Sandlin *et al.* are using 'school' and 'schooling' in their US sense to encompass all institutional education, not just pre-college, pre-university schools, as in the UK convention.
4 For a comprehensive edited collection on public pedagogy, comprising some 65 chapters, see Sandlin *et al.* (2010); and for a far-reaching overview of 420 sources, see Sandlin *et al.* (2011).
5 As I argued in Cole (2018a, 48–49), 'race' is a social construct. That this is the case is explained succinctly by neuroscientist Steven Rose and sociologist Hilary Rose (Rose and Rose, 2005; see also Darder and Torres, 2004, pp. 1–12, 25–34). As Rose and Rose note, in 1972 the evolutionary geneticist Richard Lewontin pointed out that 85 per cent of human genetic diversity occurred within, rather

than between, populations, and only 6–10 per cent of diversity is associated with the broadly defined 'races'. Rose and Rose explain that most of this difference is accounted for by the readily visible genetic variation of skin colour, hair form and so on. The everyday business of seeing and acknowledging such difference is not the same as the project of genetics. For genetics, and more importantly, for the prospect of treating genetic diseases, the difference is important, since humans differ in their susceptibility to particular diseases, and genetics can have something to say about this. However, beyond medicine, the invocation of 'race' is increasingly suspect. There has been a growing debate among geneticists, I pointed out, about the utility of the term, and an entire issue of the influential journal *Nature Reviews Genetics* (Autumn, 2004) was devoted to it. The geneticists agreed with most biological anthropologists that for human biology, the term 'race' is an unhelpful leftover. Rose and Rose argue that '[w]hatever arbitrary boundaries one places on any population group for the purposes of genetic research, they do not match those of conventionally defined races' (Rose and Rose, 2005). For example, the DNA of 'native' Britons contains traces of the multiple entries into the UK of occupiers and migrants. 'Race', as a scientific concept, Rose and Rose conclude, 'is well past its sell-by date' (Rose and Rose, 2005). The popular political slogan 'one race, the human race' would appear to be accurate. 'Race' as a concept should be abandoned. For these reasons, following Marxist sociologist Robert Miles, if I need to use the term 'race' as an 'idea', as a social construct, I put it in inverted commas. As Miles explains:

> I am rigorous in believing that there is a very clear distinction between an idea and a concept ... insofar as there is an idea of 'race' that is a historical reality ... [I] use the notion of racialization [the false categorisation of people into distinct 'races'] to then seek to explain the origin, development and use of that idea.
>
> (Ashe and McGeever, 2011)

The Marxist concept of racialization is discussed in Chapter 1 of this book.

6 The economic and political backdrop to the ascendancy of Donald Trump is discussed in Cole (2019, 45–47).

7 No previous US presidents have had a state visit to the UK in their first year in the White House. As it turned out, Trump's UK visit was downgraded to an *official* visit because of mass objections, while the visit itself was mired by angry protests from which Trump was shielded.

8 Thatcher also, of course, had an ideological affinity with May on immigration, having used her public pedagogy, which included on one occasion the adjective 'hostile', to threaten prospective immigrants, also in the context of getting the numbers down:

> if we went on as we are then by the end of the century there would be four million people of the new Commonwealth or Pakistan here. Now, that is an awful lot and I think it means that people are really rather afraid that this country might be rather swamped by people with a different culture and, you know, the British character has done so much for democracy, for law and done so much throughout the world that if there is any fear that it might be swamped people are going to react and be rather *hostile* to those coming in.
>
> (Margaret Thatcher Foundation, 1978; emphasis added)

This was, of course, a classic example of playing 'the "race" card'.

1 Immigration and the hostile environment

Backdrop, creation and consolidation

> My aim is to 'weed out' those who do not deserve to be here … and 'to create here in Britain a really hostile environment'.
>
> (Theresa May, Speech on Immigration, 5 November 2010 … Interview with the *Telegraph*, 25 May 2015)

Introduction

In this first chapter, I begin by addressing the economic and political backdrop to the 'really hostile environment', initiated by Theresa May, then Home Secretary, in May 2012. Its genesis needs to be seen in the light of the financial crash of 2007–2008 and the onset of the Great Recession, followed by the austerity measures implemented first by a Tory-led coalition, and then by the Conservative Party itself. In order to make sense of the relationship between austerity and the hostile environment, forged in a blanket public pedagogy of hate around the issue of immigration, and the deployment by the Tories of 'the "race" card' in the lead-up to the 2010 General Election (that resulted in the ConDem coalition Government), I introduce the Marxist concept of racialization. Having set this toxic background, I move on to an analysis of the naming, creation and consolidation by May of the hostile environment itself. This entailed the fostering of a most reactionary climate of fear directed at some of the UK's most vulnerable people. The hostile environment is accompanied by draconian policies, regulations, legislation and rules, centred around May's ideological and political obsession with reducing net annual migration to below one-hundred-thousand, and to be the one to herald the permanent cessation of free movement of workers. I focus in this chapter on May's stewardship of the Home Office. In so doing, I note key changes in family migration rules, May's controversial 'go home vans' and her moving of the second reading of the Immigration Bill in 2013. The subsequent 2014 Act is viewed in the context of ongoing racism in the run-up to the 2015 General Election, a racism that I demonstrate was not confined to the Tory Party. The result of the election was an outright majority for the Tories under Cameron, who a few months before had said he would not serve a third term as Prime Minister. This decision, as we shall see in Chapter 2, projected Theresa May to Number 10, in what turned out to be one of the most fragile and turbulent premierships in UK political history.

The 'really hostile environment': economic and political backdrop

The global financial crisis 2007–2008, and the onset of the Great Recession 2008–2013

What follows is a timeline of the global financial crisis and the onset of the Great Recession, with particular emphasis on the UK (adapted from Kingsley, 2012).[1]

9 August 2007: French International Banking Group BNP Paribas becomes the first major bank to acknowledge the risk of exposure to sub-prime mortgage (issued at high interest rates to borrowers with low credit ratings) markets. Adam Applegarth, British bank, Northern Rock's chief executive, later said that it was 'the day the world changed'.

14 September 2007: Having borrowed large sums of money to fund customers' mortgages, Northern Rock needs to pay off its debt by reselling those mortgages in the international capital markets. But, given that the demand had fallen, it faces a liquidity (cash flow) crisis and needs a Government loan, sparking fears that it would soon go bankrupt. Customers queue round the block to withdraw their savings, the first run on a British bank for 150 years.

17 February 2008: After the failure of two private takeover bids, Labour Chancellor of the Exchequer in the Gordon Brown Government, Alistair Darling nationalizes Northern Rock, stating it is to be a temporary measure. It will be nearly four years before it is re-privatized.

7 September 2008: The US government bails out Fannie Mae and Freddie Mac – two huge firms that had guaranteed thousands of sub-prime mortgages.

15 September 2008: Heavily exposed to the sub-prime mortgage market, the American bank Lehman Brothers files for bankruptcy, prompting worldwide financial panic.

17 September 2008: The UK's largest mortgage lenders, HBOS, is taken over by Lloyds TSB after a huge drop in its share price.

30 September 2008: Shortly after becoming the first European country to slide into recession, Ireland's government promises to underwrite the entire Irish banking system – a pledge it will ultimately be unable to uphold.

8 October 2008: Amid the worst ever week for the Dow Jones Index, eight central banks including the Bank of England, the European Central Bank, and the Federal Reserve cut their interest rates by 0.5 per cent in a coordinated attempt to ease the pressure on borrowers.

13 October 2008: To avert the collapse of the UK banking sector, the British government bails out several banks, including the Royal Bank of Scotland, Lloyds TSB, and HBOS.

20 April 2009: The G20 (the international forum for the governments and central bank governors from 19 countries and the European Union) agrees on a global stimulus package worth $5 trillion.

The crisis and ensuing major recession had an enduring ideological impact:

Everything that the politicians and economists and bankers had told their populations for two decades about the superiority of free markets turned out to be false. Free markets, it appeared, were responsible instead for the devastation of the world economy. The blatant white collar crime[2] revealed in the most respectable banks only added to the ideological turmoil. No longer could the ruling class just dismiss critics of the 'free market' as throwbacks to an old and superseded order. For the first time, criticisms of the neoliberal order were published on a regular basis in the leading organs of the world's press.

(Bramble, 2018)

Despite this, the ruling class claimed no alternative to the dominant public pedagogy favouring neoliberalism (Margaret Thatcher's key mantra had been 'there is no alternative' or TINA – as we shall see this was repeated in essence by Osborne in 2010, and in actuality by Cameron in 2013) while the public pedagogy of oppositional groups did not at the time carry enough weight to be taken seriously. Thus, as Tom Bramble (2018), Marxist scholar and long-time political activist concludes, the ruling class was able to impose ruthless austerity as a way out of the crisis:

> Whatever their differences, the ruling classes could agree on one basic point in the aftermath of the immediate crisis: that the working class, as during every capitalist crisis, had to pay for the cost of rescuing the system.... For the first time in many decades, people in the West could expect their children to have a lower standard of living than themselves.

At this point, in order to make connections between austerity and racism, I turn to the *Marxist* concept of racialization (the term is used in different ways by non-Marxists).

The Marxist concept of racialization

Robert Miles (1987) has defined racialization as an ideological process that accompanies the appropriation of labour power (the capacity to labour), where people are categorized falsely into the scientifically defunct notion of distinct 'races'. Racialization, like racism, is socially constructed. In Miles' (1989, p. 75) words, racialization refers to

> those instances where social relations between people have been struc-tured by the signification of human biological characteristics [else-where in the same book, Miles (1989, p. 79) has added cultural characteristics] in such a way as to define and *construct* differentiated social collectivities.

(1989, 75; emphasis added)

'[T]he process of racialization', Miles states, 'cannot be adequately under-stood without a conception of, and explanation for the complex interplay of different modes of production and, in particular, of the social relations necessarily established in the course of material production' (Miles 1987, p. 7). This articulation with modes of production makes the concept of racialization inherently Marxist.

Miles (1987, p. 75) argues that racialization is not limited to skin colour. The characteristics signified vary historically and, although they have usually been visible somatic features, other non-visible (alleged and real) biological features have also been signified. He stresses that racialization is a process and recognition that 'opens the door to history' which subsequently 'opens the door to understanding the complexities of who gets racialized when and for what purpose, and how that changes through time' (in Ashe and McGeever, 2011, p. 2019). Miles warns against avoiding the 'fundamental mistake' of drawing clear lines between what happens to white immigrants and black immigrants, adding that the 'black–white' dichotomy leads you into a 'huge cul-de-sac' (in Ashe and McGeever, 2011, p. 2019).

I would want to make an amendment to Miles' definition. The common dictionary definition of 'somatic' is '*pertaining to the body*', and, given the fact that people can be racialized on grounds of symbols (e.g. the hijab), I would also argue that this needs to be recognized in any discussion of social collectivities and the construction of racialization.

Elsewhere (e.g. Cole, 2016, chapter 1; 2018a, 2018b; see also Cole and Maisuria, 2014; Tomlinson, 2019; Virdee, 2014), I have analysed the many manifestations of racism in the UK, its continuities and changing nature, dating back to the colonial era, through history and in the present. These multifarious forms of racism include older-colour-coded racism (anti-Chinese racism; and racism directed at Asian, black and other minority ethnic communities; see Cole, 1993 for a discussion of this nomenclature); older non-colour-coded racism (anti-Irish racism; antisemitism; and anti-Gypsy Roma and Traveller racism) in addition to newer non-colour-coded racism (xeno-racism – defined later in this chapter) and newer hybridist racism (Islamophobia and anti-asylum seeker racism). I use the term, 'hybridist' to refer to those forms of racism that can be colour-coded, non-colour-coded or a combination of both (see Cole, 2018a, 78–87).

For my purposes in this book, it is necessary to stress that the public pedagogy of hate associated with Theresa May's 'really hostile environment', is directed in political rhetoric at recent (potential) 'immigrants' in general and at 'asylum seekers', although, as we shall see in Chapters 4 and 5, the hostile environment also targets black and other UK citizens. As such, the intensification of racism unleashed by May can be colour-coded or non-colour-coded or hybridist. This is important to point out, since claims are made that being worried about immigration is not racist and that it is not possible to be racist towards white European citizens, whereas, of course, it is. Racism directed at white people is not new and has a long history in the UK (Cole, 2018a, 65–73).

Re-launch of 'the "race" card': the lead-up to the 2010 General Election

In 2009, the Westminster MPs' expenses scandal (Grice, 2009) must have surely fuelled public scepticism of the 'them and us' state of affairs between the bankers and their political backers on the one hand, and the effect on the workers of the financial crisis and the Great Recession, on the other. All this was just a foretaste of the divisions that were to be created by the dramatic austerity measures aimed squarely at the working class that were unleashed after the general election.

In the European Elections on 4 June 2009, the racist anti-immigration, United Kingdom Independence Party (UKIP) claimed a political break-through, the party having gained four extra MEPs to take its total number of seats in the European Parliament to 13 – the same number as Labour, having pushed out Labour to take second place in the overall share of the vote – some 16.5 per cent, or 2.49 million votes (Whitehead, 2009). Labour's percentage was 15.7. The then UKIP leader Nigel Farage, a high profile 'man of the people' (pint of beer and cigarette in hand) and future enthusiast of, and campaigner for, Donald Trump (Wilson, 2017), denied it was a result of the expenses scandal and said of the results that Labour's broken promise on an EU referendum led to the rout, and called on Labour Prime Minister Gordon Brown to step down since he had 'beaten him in a national election' (cited in Whitehead, 2009):

> According to all the experts, this is the second fluke in a row that we have produced. People vote for us because they agree with us. They agree with us that we should be friendly with Europe, trade with Europe, be good neighbours, but not have our laws made there. We have managed to move on from a result five years ago that was considered to be the high water mark. We are up on those elections. We have done extremely well. We have come second nationally. We are very happy people.
>
> (Cited in Whitehead, 2009)

The fascist British National Party got 6.2 per cent of the vote, and the far-right English Democrats, 1.8 per cent, giving a combined racist anti-immigration vote for the hard Eurosceptic right-wing to far right[3] UKIP, the BNP and the English Democrats of nearly one quarter of the votes (24.5 per cent), not far behind the Conservatives at 27.7 per cent (*BBC News*, 2009). UKIP, as we shall see, was to be most significant in the creation of the hostile environment, and the subsequent racist trajectory of the Tory Party.

Racism serves the 'divide-and-rule' tactics of capitalism in diverse ways, and directs workers' attention away from their real enemy and towards their racialized sisters and brothers. This was recognized by Marx towards the end of the nineteenth century:

> In all the big industrial centres in England there is profound antago-nism between the Irish proletariat and the English proletariat. The average English worker hates the Irish worker as a competitor who lowers wages and the standard of life. He feels national and religious antipathies for him. He regards him somewhat like the poor whites of the Southern states regard their black slaves. This antagonism among the proletarians of England is artificially nourished and supported by the bourgeoisie. It knows that this scission is the true secret of maintaining its power.
>
> (Marx, 1870 [1978], p. 254)

In the harsh economic and political climate of the lead-up to the 2010 Election, the Tories clearly had to steal the mantle of racism from UKIP, and the obvious way to do that was to play 'the "race" card'. On 10 January 2010, David Cameron, then Leader of the Opposition, stated:

> We would like to see net immigration in the tens of thousands rather than the hundreds of thousands. I don't think that's unrealistic. That's the sort of figure it was in the 1990s and I think we should see that again.
>
> (Cited in Prince, 2010)

Despite there being a long history of racism in the Conservative Party (e.g. Maisuria, 2006), political journalist for the pro-Tory *Telegraph*, Rosa Prince (2010) points out that, in the years immediately preceding 2010, the Tories had shied away from putting the issue of immigration at the centre of the party's election campaigning. This was for fear of appearing as the 'nasty party', ironically a term reiterated by Theresa May in 2002 when, as newly appointed Chair of the Conservative Party, she stunned conference delegates by denunciating past sins – still 'unrepentant, just plain unat-tractive' – admitting:

> let's not kid ourselves. There's a way to go before we can return to government. There's a lot we need to do in this party of ours. Our base is too narrow and so, occasionally, are our sympathies. You know what some people call us: the nasty party.
>
> (Cited in White and Perkins, 2002)

As former *Guardian* political editor, Michael White and deputy editor, Ann Perkins (2002) clarify, as well as corruption and 'incestuous feuding', the party had suffered two major electoral setbacks. Freelance journalist Aleks Eror (2018) notes:

> Still traumatised by a second consecutive landslide defeat against the Labour Party, then headed by Tony Blair, the Tories had come together to plot their return to government after five long years out of power ... Theresa May ... took to the stage in an all-black outfit that added to the funereal atmosphere.

The party had also been accused of the exclusion of women and minority ethnic MPs. In her conference address, May referred to unnamed colleagues trying to 'make political capital out of demonising minorities':

> At the last general election 38 new Tory MPs were elected. Of that total only one was a woman and none was from an ethnic minority. Is that fair? Is one half of the population entitled to only one place out of 38?
>
> (Cited in White and Perkins, 2002)

By 2010, however, the time was ripe to bring back immigration centre-stage. As Prince (2010) explains, by then Conservative chiefs felt that voters were 'keen to hear more about limiting the numbers arriving from overseas'. This perception was not confined to the Tories. Frank Field, a former Labour welfare minister (then a Labour MP, now Independent, but traditionally socially conservative and one of Margaret Thatcher's 'closest personal friends on the Labour benches', *Liverpool Echo*, 2013), and Nicholas Soames, a Conservative backbencher, who were members of an all-party group on immigration, welcomed Cameron's January 10 initiative. In a joint statement, they stated: 'We welcome this statement from the Conservatives and hope the Government will follow suit, and that both parties carry manifesto commitments in this year's general election to keep our population below 70 million' (cited in Prince, 2010).

The ConDem Government: first year of office – 2010–2011

The 2010 election took place on 6 May and resulted in a hung parliament, with the Conservatives winning 307 seats, Labour 258, Liberal Democrats 57, the Northern Irish Democratic Unionist Party (DUP) 6, Scottish National Party (SNP) 5 and Others 14 (*BBC Election*, 2010). A superficial estimate of who might form a coalition would point to the nominally left-of-centre parties, Labour and the Liberal Democrats. However, with the

Tories as big gainers and Labour as big losers, the odds were essentially tipped against a Labour/Lib Dem coalition, not least since it would have depended on the support of smaller groups on a day-to-day basis to win Commons votes (Riddell, 2010). What led to a coalition between the Conservatives and the Liberal Democrats, formed just after midnight on 12 May, however, was decided by a combination of factors, as outlined by Peter Riddell (2010), who draws on analyses by two MPs, David Laws (Laws, 2010), a key member of the Liberal Democrat negotiating team, and Rob Wilson (Wilson, 2010), a Conservative Whip at the time. The reasons, as Riddell points out, were complicated, but one key factor was that a younger generation of prominent Lib Dem politicians, notably Nick Clegg who was shortly to become Deputy Prime Minister, were less hostile to the Conservatives than the 'older generation' of leaders, who tended to be more 'centre-left'. This made them more open from the start to Cameron's 'big, open and comprehensive offer', made shortly after the election result. Another element was the fact that 'the Tories', with a few notable exceptions, 'were hungrier for power almost on any terms than a tired Labour team' (Riddell, 2010). David Cameron became Prime Minister and Theresa May, Home Secretary and Minister for Women and Equalities. The inappropriateness of this latter role, given the negative effect of the hostile environment on domestic violence, and the number of women in the divided families that May created, will become apparent in this book (see, in particular, Chapters 3 and 4).

Immigration limitation becomes key policy

The Coalition Agreement of May 2010 included the following (it is common practice in party politics to say something positive before the main negative intention of the speaker is revealed):

> The Government believes that immigration has enriched our culture and strengthened our economy, but that it must be controlled so that people have confidence in the system. We also recognise that to ensure cohesion and protect our public services, we need to introduce a cap on immigration and reduce the number of non-EU immigrants. We will introduce an annual limit on the number of non-EU economic migrants admitted into the UK to live and work.[4]
>
> (The Coalition: Our programme for Government, 2010, 21)

As well as the re-emergence of 'the "race" card' per se in Tory Party politics and the Cameron 'tens of thousands' aspiration, this statement also needs to be viewed in the context of the fact that while the United Kingdom Independence Party (UKIP) had failed to turn its European Election success in 2009 into a UK General Election one (16.5 per cent vote share in the former; and 3.2 per cent in the latter) (Hunt, 2014), and although it did not win any seats in parliament, UKIP's performance was, at the time, the best performance by any minor party in a UK election (Bogdanor, 2012).

When Michael Pearson stepped down as UKIP leader in August 2010, announcing that he did not enjoy party politics (Hunt, 2014), Farage once again became UKIP's leader (he had previously held that office from 2006 to 2009). In his leadership acceptance speech on 5 November 2010, Farage immediately launched into David Cameron for what he saw as Cameron's retreat over the Referendum, a 'no' vote on continuing membership of the EU by the people being axiomatic to UKIP in reducing immigration:

> His international policy for the United Kingdom is simple – it is surrender, surrender, surrender. Patriotic eurosceptic Tories are beginning to realise that under David Cameron ... their party has ceased to exist. Quite simply, they have given up. Remember the cast-iron pledge we had from the prime minister? 'I give you this pledge, there will be a referendum on the Lisbon treaty'. Well of course, he turned his back on that. The only party prepared to talk about these issues openly, the only party prepared to put these great questions about who governs Britain to a referendum is now Ukip.
>
> (Cited in Sparrow, 2010)

Austerity is unleashed

On 20 October 2010, the *Financial Times* revealed what it referred to as 'the most drastic budget cuts in living memory, outstripping measures taken by other advanced economies which are also under pressure to sharply reduce public spending' (Pimlott *et al.*, 2010). This ushering in of a 'new age of austerity' had been promised by Cameron some 18 months before the ConDem October 2010 announcement (Summers, 2009). The sweeping cuts in spending and entitlements amounted to £81 billion over four years – the equivalent of 4.5 per cent of projected 2014–2015 gross domestic product (Pimlott *et al.*, 2010).

Declaring that 'today is the day where Britain steps back from the brink', Chancellor of the Exchequer, George Osborne promised a £7 billion fall in welfare support and 490,000 public sector job cuts by 2014–2015. Reflecting the Tory TINA ideology (Maisuria, 2018), Osborne insisted that there is no alternative to making the working class pay for the bankers' crisis: 'Tackling the budget deficit is unavoidable. To back down now and abandon our plans would be the road to economic ruin' (cited in Pimlott *et al.*, 2010). Local government was particularly targeted with reductions of nearly 30 per cent by 2015, while the police force saw its budget trimmed by 16 per cent (two areas – the science budget and overseas aid were protected). Osborne confirmed that the government was raising the state pension age from 65 to 66 for men from 2020 (Pimlott *et al.*, 2010).

Given this degree of austerity that *condemned* the working class as a whole to varying degrees of poverty and desperation and misery (e.g. Portes, 2018; Booth and Butler, 2018), this emerging alliance of Tories and Liberal Democrats can be appropriately abbreviated to ConDem (Cole, 2012, 5).

Home Secretary May enters the fray and wades in on immigration

Such open and blatant class warfare from above (Hill, 2019) was in urgent need of a scapegoat. Enter Theresa May into the fray with her first major speech on immigration, significantly made on the same day as Farage's attack on Cameron (5 November 2010). Describing it as 'one of the most important issues facing our country' (GOV.UK, 2010), May began with the usual softener – 'managed well, immigration is something that can bring great benefits' – then launched into an offensive against (prospective) migrants by continuing, '[but] managed poorly, it is something that can cause great economic and social pressure', and the 'government is committed to reducing the number of non-EU migrants'. 'Net inward migration in the last year', May went on, 'was nearly 200,000'. Upping the alarmist public pedagogy, she stated, 'Between 1997 and 2009, net migration to Britain totalled more than 2.2 million people. That is more than twice the population of Birmingham' (GOV.UK, 2010). May then mentioned 'stories of abuse of the system', before referring to 'serious social impacts in some areas, with pressure being placed on key public services such as schools, the health service, transport, housing and welfare'.

It is a convenient convention for (right-wing) governments to falsely blame immigrants for putting pressure on public services (e.g. Chakrabortty, 2018), rather than privatization and lack of government funding, both part of ongoing neoliberalization (e.g. Maisuria and Cole, 2017). Moreover, crucially May was, as a cabinet minister, complicit in the ideological *choice* to impose austerity on the working class and make them pay for the bailout of the banks, following the 2007/2008 financial crisis.[5]

In a direct and assertive exercise in public pedagogy, May then alluded to 'the segregation we see in too many of our communities' that 'created community tensions and helped contribute to a society that is not as integrated as we would like', before pledging: 'The public should know that I will take action. I am determined to get the immigration system back under control' (GOV.UK, 2010).

This callous public pedagogy of hate, blame and threat: 'immigrants create segregation and community tension and we will take action to control them' belies the fact that an alternative to denouncing immigrants and trying to make them pay psychologically and financially to earn the right to be in the UK, is to welcome them in various ways into our communities and to value the various contributions that they make.

Comparing controlling immigration using the 'points-based system alone' (where applicants must reach a points score above a minimum threshold to be successful) to 'squeezing a balloon', she spewed further scaremongering, emotive and hostile rhetoric:

> *Push down* work visas and the number of student visas will *shoot up.* *Clamp down* on student visas and family visas will *spring up. Bear down* on family visas and work visas will *explode.* With unskilled labour set to zero, all that happened was student visas *rocketed by thirty per cent to a record 304,000 in just one year*, as some applicants used it as an alternative work route.
>
> (GOV.UK, 2010; emphases added)

Making a direct pitch for immigration from capitalists and highly qualified scientists – 'the brightest and the best' – and the need to keep out impoverished workers, May proclaimed: 'We can increase the number of high value migrants: the entrepreneurs, the investors, the research scientists – at the same time as we reduce the total number of people coming to Britain through the economic routes' (GOV.UK, 2010).

After revealing measures for the economic route, with further reference to 'cracking down', May moved on to the education route, promising a 'more robust system ... to ensure [students'] departure at the end of their legitimate stay'; she proclaimed:

> People might imagine that by students we mean people who come here for a few years to study at university and then go home – but that's not always the case. We estimate that nearly half of all students coming here from abroad are coming to study a course below degree level. We have to question whether these are the brightest and the best that Britain wants to attract – they may be, or they may not.
>
> (GOV.UK, 2010)

She then compared the education route to the economic, using further hostile public pedagogy of hate:

We will follow exactly the same principle as in the skilled work route – a more selective approach, which attracts the highly skilled, the talented and the genuinely needed, but reduces numbers overall by *weeding out those who do not deserve to be allowed in*. The *sheer number* of students coming in, and the large proportion of total inward migration this represents, means we cannot delay in taking this *necessary and decisive action.*

(GOV.UK, 2010; emphases added)

While this makes party political 'sense', given government intentions to pander to popular racism within the confines of the 'logic' of capitalism, there is a contradiction. Capitalism values entrepreneurs because they create the conditions for the extraction of surplus values from workers by setting up capitalist enterprise, but it also aims to drive down wages to increase surplus value, and immigrants historically are a source of cheap labour.[6] Hence, there are often competing demands between politicians playing 'the "race" card' and capitalists hungry for low-paid workers. Thus, in an interview on the *BBC News* Channel on 19 November 2018, Josh Hardie, Confederation of British Industry (CBI) Deputy Director-General stressed the need for lower-skilled workers as well as entrepreneurs.

Widening the net of her targeted scapegoats, May's alarmist and hostile rhetoric blamed immigration once again for the decline in 'public services', which she obviously knew was about to increase dramatically with the onset of austerity:

uncontrolled immigration is bad for our economy and it is bad for our society. It puts pressure on the public services that people rely on and creates unnecessary tension and discord. I want a more selective approach which prioritises our universities, attracts the brightest and best workers and minimises abuse in the study and family routes … I want to bear down on all the routes into Britain and to crack down on abuse of the system. We will cap the number of economic migrants from outside the EU and ensure only those workers who are genuinely needed for our economy are allowed in. We will reduce the numbers of bogus students coming here to study. And we will strengthen controls on family visas.

(GOV.UK, 2010)

May concluded by repeating Cameron's infamous and unrealistic pledge to drastically reduce the immigration of *workers* into the UK to the tens of thousands, by claiming that only the rich deserve to migrate to the UK:

For all these routes, I want a clear way to control who can settle in Britain – that is a historic privilege that we should not fritter away lightly. I want the message to go out loud and clear that Britain will remain open for business. Our economy will remain accessible to the best and the brightest in the world, that's why, as the Prime Minister said yesterday, entrepreneurs will be welcome; scientists will be welcome; wealth creators will be welcome. But we must make sure that migration is properly controlled. We will reduce net migration from the hundreds of thousands to the tens of thousands. It will not be easy. It will take hard work and a great deal of political courage. But the British people want us to do it and it is the right thing to do. So we will do it.

(GOV.UK, 2010)

May's offensive against the 'immigrant family'

A central plank of May's offensive was directed at the family, as constituted of a British and foreign spouse/civil partner; engaged (with plans to marry within six months) or who have been living together in a relationship for two years. 'An area where we have already taken action', she asserted,

> is the family visa route. Unsurprisingly perhaps, over two-thirds of the 63,000 people who entered the UK in 2004 to join family here, were still in Britain five years later. And last year, some 40,000 marriage visas were issued.
>
> (GOV.UK, 2010)

'We estimate', May went on, 'that the family route accounted for nearly 20 per cent of non EU migration last year'. Heralding what was later to crystallize into that part of the 'really hostile environment' that was to divide families, this clergy's daughter, singling out an imprisoned cleric, threatened and warned:

> This summer, we ordered the UK Border Agency to clamp down on sham marriages. They have had significant success, conducting 53 operations and making 118 arrests. Shockingly, this included the arrest of a vicar who was subsequently jailed for staging over 300 sham marriages. As well as tackling abuse of the marriage route we need to ensure that those who come here can integrate successfully into society and play a part in their local community. So from 29 November, those applying for marriage visas will have to demonstrate

a minimum standard of English. This is only right. People coming to this country must be able to interact with the rest of the population.

May added: 'And we need to go further. We must look at measures to tighten this route, for example by introducing processes to allow us to check that the UK sponsor is able to maintain and accommodate the foreign spouse' (cited in GOV.UK, 2010). Referring to 'temporary versus permanent migration', she promised that 'No one is suggesting that those who come here to marry legitimately should not be able to make the UK their permanent home' (GOV.UK, 2010). The reality is that she went on to make this as difficult as she possibly could.

Just over two weeks later (23 November 2010), May's resolve to play 'the "race" card' was repeated to the House of Commons (www. parliament.uk, 2014) and reiterated by Cameron in April 2011, when he said that he had:

> made a clear commitment to the British people that we would aim to reduce net migration to the levels we saw in the 1980s and 1990s. Now we are in government, we are on track to meet that aim.
>
> (www.parliament.uk, 2014)

Theresa May names, creates and consolidates the 'really hostile environment'

The public pedagogy of 'real hostility' becomes enshrined in government policy

The public pedagogy of hostility was heralded and enshrined in government policy in an interview with the *Telegraph* on 25 May 2012, when Theresa May, having been Home Secretary and Minister for Women and Equality for just over two years, announced, 'The aim is to create here in Britain a really hostile environment for illegal migration' (cited in Kirkup and Winnett, 2012).[7] As a prelude to the plan to turn landlords, health workers and other public sector workers into border guards, she explained: 'What we don't want is a situation where people think that they can come here and overstay because they're able to access everything they need' (cited in Kirkup and Winnett, 2012). Although May referred to so-called '*illegal* immigration', irrespective of her intentions, the hostile environment has served to encourage people in the UK to be both hostile towards and to fear (prospective) immigrants *in general*, and to instil fear and terror in the hearts and minds of those migrants in the UK and those wishing to come to the UK.

As the *Guardian* Home Affairs correspondent Jamie Grierson (2018) argues, only May knew at the time whether the 'hostile environment' strategy – 'essentially empowering figures across society to become immigration enforcement officers – would evolve into a catch-all brand for her approach to migrants, illegal or otherwise' because ' "the hostile environment" came to encapsulate not just her approach to illegal immigration but to reflect a broader rancour towards migrants in the UK'.

Official figures at the time of the interview showed that net immigration was running at about 250,000 a year, well above the 'tens of thousands' that Conservatives (but not the Lib Dems) promised that the ConDem government would deliver (Kirkup and Winnett, 2012).

With respect to that part of the 'really hostile environment' that was used to create divided families (see Chapter 4 of this book), in a diatribe against 'sham marriages and sham civil partnerships' in her speech on the second reading of the Immigration Bill in October 2013, Theresa May stated that the Home Office estimated at the time that between 4,000 and 10,000 applications to stay in the UK are made on the basis of unions 'undertaken by a fraudulent couple for their own immigration advantage'. May pointed out that registration officials already had a duty to report 'suspected sham marriages and sham civil partnerships to the Home Office', and the number of reported cases had risen in recent years, with 1,891 reports received in 2012. She continued with a public pedagogy of threat and cruelty, so cold-hearted that it is difficult to believe that May is talking about fellow human beings:

> At the moment we have the ridiculous situation where we cannot always stop a marriage or civil partnership that a registrar believes to be a sham. The current 15-day notice period provides very little time for the Home Office to act before the ceremony takes place. This Bill will increase the marriage and civil partnership notice period to 28 days in England and Wales. It also allows for it to be extended to 70 days where we have reasonable grounds to suspect that a marriage or civil partnership is a sham. The Home Office will investigate the genuineness of the couple's relationship and consider taking immigration enforcement action where we believe it to be a sham. *If the couple do not comply with the investigation, we will stop a marriage from taking place. Should a sham marriage or civil partnership go ahead, couples will not gain an immigration advantage. They will be removed or prosecuted.*
>
> (GOV.UK, 2013; emphasis added)

Contra May's contempt for immigrants and a lack of consideration and concern that a couple in love may object to being 'investigated', there is, of course, a *moral* case that marriages based not on love, but on compassion, where one partner provides economic, emotional or other forms of security, or sanctuary from mental or physical harm out of genuine human decency, could be lauded as exemplary acts of authentic human kindness.

Draconian changes in family migration rules; then Cameron champions the working-class family

In July 2012, key changes to family migration rules came into force. These draconian, vicious and callous assaults on (working-class) family life[8] have been summarized by Richmond Chambers Immigration Barristers (2012) and include:

Spouses and partners
- Spouses, civil partners, unmarried partners and same sex partners of people who are British or settled in the UK now have to complete five years of limited leave to remain in this category before they are eligible for indefinite leave to remain. The five years will be made up of two periods of two and a half years each;
- Since October 2013, spouses and partners applying for indefinite leave to remain will need to pass both the Life in the UK Test and an English test at level B1;
- Spouses or partners who have been married to or living with the British or settled person outside the UK for four years are no longer able to get indefinite leave to enter or remain immediately. They need to wait for five years;
- There must be at least £18,600 per year available to the couple. This can be made up of savings, pension or gross income from employment/self-employment (prior to 2012, there was only a requirement that the couple had enough to live on);
- If the spouse or partner is not already in the UK with an entitlement to work at the date of the application, they are not able to rely on their own predicted income from employment in the UK;
- If the couple are relying on income from employment, then they need to have had the job for at least six months before the date of application;
- The couple can only rely on savings if they have at least £16,000 and have held this for at least six months;
- It will not be possible to rely on offers of financial support from family and/or friends;
- There is a new list of factors that the UK Border Agency (UKBA) will take into account when assessing whether a relationship is genuine [see Immigration Directorate, 2012].

Children
- Children who are eligible for indefinite leave to enter will continue to have to meet the current requirements of the Immigration Rules;
- Children who are being granted limited leave only (because only one parent is settled in the UK and they are applying with the other parent) have to show that there is an extra £3,800 per year for the first child and £2,400 per year for each additional child.

Adult dependent relatives
- The only dependent relatives over 18 who can apply will be parents, grandparents, children and siblings;
- The dependent relative has to show that because of age, illness or disability they require long-term personal care;
- The required care must be unavailable in the relative's home country even with the UK sponsor's financial assistance, because it is not affordable or there is no one to provide it;
- It is not possible to apply under this category from inside the UK.

Human rights and discretionary leave to remain
- People granted leave to remain on human rights grounds will not have recourse to public funds;
- Limited leave to remain on human rights grounds will be granted for two and a half years at once;
- A person will have to complete ten years of human rights-based leave before they are eligible for indefinite leave to remain;
- Leave to remain based on private life in the UK will usually only be granted after a person has lived in the UK for 20 years' residence (for adults), seven years (for children), more than half their life (if they are aged 18 to 25). It may be granted earlier if the person has no ties with their home country;
- The Immigration Rules will set out what the United Kingdom UKBA believes to be in the 'public interest' in Article 8 claims based on private and/or family life in the UK;
- The '14-year rule', whereby people can get indefinite leave to remain after living in the UK for 14 years, is abolished (Richmond Chambers Immigration Barristers, 2012[9]).

Cameron invokes TINA

Early the following the year (7 March 2013) Cameron invoked TINA, in a bid to champion austerity as the saviour of the working-class family: 'If there was another way I would take it. But there is no alternative' (cited in Robinson, 2013). Also reminiscent of Thatcher, Cameron drew on the familial interpellation[10] to impress on the working class that their sacrifices will ultimately reap benefits:

> I know things are tough right now. Families are struggling with the bills at the end of the month. Some are just a pay-cheque away from going into the red. Parents are worried about what the future holds for their children. Whole towns are wondering where their economic future lies. And I know that is especially true for people here in York-shire and in many parts of the north of our country who didn't benefit properly from the so-called boom years and worry they won't do so again. But I'm here to say that's not going to happen. Because we have a plan to get through these difficulties – and to get through them together.
>
> (Cited in Robinson, 2013)

May toughens up the message on the vans: 'go home or face arrest'

Between 22 July and 22 August 2013, vans were sent by Theresa May's Home Office into six London boroughs with high minority ethnic popula-tions. As Simon Hattenstone (2018) explains, the pilot operation was to test the hypothesis that people without leave to remain would depart vol-untarily if they were made aware of 'a near and present' danger of being arrested. He goes on, the pilot is best remembered for the message, 'In the UK illegally? Go home or face arrest' (Hattenstone, 2018). Underneath the threatening question was a picture of a handcuff, and to the right the pur-ported number of arrests in that particular area. Under the main message was the invitation to 'Text HOME to 78070 for free advice, and help with travel documents', and underneath that, 'We can help you to return home voluntarily without fear of arrest or detention'.

Hattenstone points out that other Home Office operations over the years were often given simple neutral names taken from nature, rather than being related to the case in question. This particular one, however, was named Operation Vaken. According to Sally Tomlinson (2019, 189), it was named after a poem promoting fascism in 1930s Germany. Posters were also placed in minority ethnic newspapers, and in mosques and temples urging people to 'Go Home'. Detention of immigrants increased, although four in ten appeals against detention were successful (Tomlinson, 2019, 189).

According to political reporter Thomas Colson and political editor Adam Bienkov (Colson and Bienkov, 2018) of *Business Insider*, May and her special advisers were sent plans and publicity images for the vans as early as March 2013. Not only did she approve the proposals, but also requested that the language of the slogans was 'toughened up' before the vans were rolled out. As Hattenstone (2018) concludes (underlining the fact that May was determined to make UKIP-style hatred central to her public pedagogies of hostility):

> Like much Home Office policy, it appeared to be a response to the then growing popularity of Ukip. If the Conservative-Lib Dem coalition was to keep Ukip at bay, it believed it would have to convince voters it was not a soft touch: that it was equally determined to reduce the number of immigrants ... Theresa May was almost obsessively determined to get the figure down to tens of thousands ... and had a zero tolerance policy to those who had no right to be in the country.

Even Farage described the tone of the billboards as 'nasty' and 'unpleasant' (*BBC News*, 2013b), while Shadow Home Secretary at the time Yvette Cooper accused the Tories of 'borrowing the language of the 1970s [fascist] National Front' (cited in Travis, 2013). Lord Kerslake, head of the civil service between 2012 and 2014, went further, stating that the whole 'hostile immigration environment Theresa May set out to create when she was at the Home Office was regarded by some ministers as "almost reminiscent of Nazi Germany" in the way it is working' (Perkins and Quinn, 2018).

The second reading of the Immigration Bill 2013

On 22 October 2013, May moved the second reading of the Immigration Bill, and in so doing pledged again to reduce immigration to the tens of thousands. She began by reaffirming the creation of the hostile and aggressive-sounding Border Force (Border Force, itself, being a brief sobriquet of the public pedagogy inherent in the 'really hostile environment').[11] At this point in the chapter, it will not be a surprise that the standard public pedagogy of hostility with respect to the 'significant problem' of immigration was deployed in abundance. Again, while 'illegal' figures prominently in the rhetoric, it would have been received by many as legitimating and encouraging hostility to all migrants and to 'foreigners' in general. Thus May ended her stark, cruel and callous diatribe of venom, her public pedagogy of 'real hostility' as follows:

> It is frankly ridiculous that the Government has to operate such a complex system to deal with *foreigners* who fail to abide by *our laws*.

It is ridiculous that the odds are stacked in favour of illegal migrants. It is unacceptable that hard working taxpayers have to compete with people who have no right to be here. This Bill will begin to address these absurdities and restore the balance.

(GOV.UK, 2013; emphases added)

The speech contained more talk of 'abuse' (twice in its first paragraph), along with 'clamping down'; 'cracking down'; 'taking advantage'; 'removals'; 'not fair to the public' who are 'fed up'. In May's words: 'This is not just about making the UK a more hostile place for illegal migrants – it is about fairness'. Having made three references to 'foreign criminals', May then coupled them with immigration lawyers: 'Under the current system the winners are foreign criminals and immigration lawyers and the losers are the victims of those crimes and the law-abiding public' (GOV. UK, 2013).

Racism and the run-up to the 7 May 2015 General Election

Mindful of Farage's blistering attack on Cameron in 2010, and the more general threat from UKIP and the need to keep the Eurosceptics in the Tory Party in line, in January 2013, in a speech six months in the planning, Cameron pledged to renegotiate the UK's relationship with the EU, followed by a simple in/out referendum. This was promised by the end of 2017 at the latest – if the Conservatives were to win the next general election on 7 May 2015. During Prime Minister's Questions, Labour Leader Ed Miliband said Mr Cameron was 'running scared' of the UK Independence Party, whose poll ratings had been rising. Cameron declared that if he managed to secure a new relationship he was happy with, he would campaign 'heart and soul' to stay within the EU (*BBC News*, 2013a).

In November 2013, Cameron announced a raft of anti-immigrant measures ahead of new EU rules that came into effect on 1 January 2014, ending restrictions on Bulgarians and Romanians entering the United Kingdom. While Eastern Europeans in general were, and are, on the receiving end of xeno-racism (that form of non-colour-coded racism directed at Eastern European workers and their families), the prime scapegoats were originally the Poles.

Former Director of the Institute of Race Relations, the late Ambalavanar Sivanandan has defined xeno-racism as follows:

It is a racism that is not just directed at those with darker skins, from the former colonial territories, but at the newer categories of the displaced, the dispossessed and the uprooted, who are beating at western Europe's doors, the Europe that helped to displace them in the first place. It is a racism, that is, that cannot be colour-coded, directed as it is at poor whites as well, and is therefore passed off as xenophobia, a 'natural' fear of strangers. But in the way it denigrates and reifies people before segregating and/or expelling them, it is a xenophobia that bears all the marks of the old racism. It is racism in substance, but 'xeno' in form. It is a racism that is meted out to impoverished strangers even if they are white. It is xeno-racism.

(Cited in Fekete, 2001)

The new rules meant the additional racialization (the categorization of people (falsely) into distinct 'races' – see Note 5 in the Introduction to this book) of Bulgarians and Romanians. Cameron's measures included no unemployment benefits for new migrants for the first three months of their stay; out-of-work welfare payments to end after six months, unless the claimant can prove they have a 'genuine prospect' of a job; new migrants not allowed to claim housing benefits immediately; and any migrant caught begging or sleeping rough to be deported and not allowed to return to the United Kingdom for a year. In addition, migrants wishing to claim benefits are subject to more restrictions. This includes a new minimum earnings threshold. Failure to meet the requirements leads to the removal of welfare benefits, including Income Support (Stevens, 2013; see Note 1 in the Introduction to this book).

The 2014 Immigration Act

The ConDem government's Immigration Act of 2014 came into effect in May of that year. Key aspects of the Act include:

- Limiting appeals against Home Office decisions from 17 to 4;
- The right to deport first and hear appeals later in certain circumstances; the right to 'respect for family and private life' should not always take precedence over public interest, which should be 'at the heart of [the court's] decisions' in immigration control and deporting foreign criminals;
- Clamping down on those who live and work in the UK illegally and take advantage of our public services; ensuring that only legal migrants have access to the labour market, health services, housing, bank accounts and driving licences;
- Penalties for employers who do not ensure that Non-EEA (European Economic Area) nationals only work as legally permitted;

- Restricting access to free NHS care to those non-EEA nationals with 'indefinite leave to remain' and those granted refugee status or humanitarian protection, thus bringing the NHS into line with government policy on access to benefits and social housing;
- Temporary migrants seeking to stay in the UK for more than six months to pay an immigration health surcharge on top of their visa fee;
- Landlords required to check the immigration status of their prospective tenants; powers to deal with 'rogue landlords' who rent homes to 'illegal immigrants';
- With respect to 'removals', create a system where only one decision is made, informing the individual that they cannot stay in the UK, and enabling Immigration Enforcement to remove them if they do not leave voluntarily;
- For illegal migrants held in immigration detention, no bail when the detainee is booked onto a flight in the next few days and there are no exceptional circumstances; no multiple repeated bail applications;
- Full rights equivalent to the police for entry clearance officers to take fingerprints before entry to the UK, and to take enforcement action;
- Simplifying the appeals procedure so that instead of appealing to an immigration judge, applicants can contact the Home Office and ask for a simple administrative review to remedy case working errors, thus resolving errors in decisions cheaply and quickly.

(GOV.UK, 2013)

The last point means that an 'independent' judge is replaced by the 'hostile' Home Office. The Immigration Act of 2014 also provided for the removal of citizenship from naturalized citizens, if their conduct is 'seriously prejudicial to the vital interests of the United Kingdom'. This could include cases involving 'national security, terrorism, espionage or taking up arms against British or allied forces' even if removing citizenship could result in their being made stateless (Salmon, 2014).

Significantly, as part of the Act, the government quietly removed a key protection from the statute books for some British residents of the Windrush generation. The Home Office *claimed* that the clause was not included because adequate protections were already in place for people who were initially granted temporary rights to remain in the UK and have stayed for decades (Taylor, 2018). Four years later, these particular British people would face detention, the denial of legal rights, and would be threatened with deportation, with some actually wrongly deported (see Chapter 4 of this book).

With respect to the provisions of the Act, Saira Grant of the Joint Council for the Welfare of Immigrants (JCWI) has argued that the Act seeks to turn landlords, health workers and other public sector workers into border guards (Electronic Immigration Network (EIN), 2014a).

A racist consensus forms[12]

In the light of the defection of several Tories to UKIP, including one on the eve of the September 2014 Tory Party Conference, as well as the switching of a major donation by one ex-Tory from the Conservatives to UKIP, and in the context of a concerted campaign of interpellation by the right wing tabloids to demonize and criminalize Eastern Europeans, the main parties tried desperately to outbid each other to establish their anti-immigrant credentials.

Yvette Cooper, at the 2014 Labour Party Conference, stated that Labour 'got things wrong on immigration – on transitional controls for Eastern Europe, on the impact on jobs'. Castigating the Tories for not reducing net immigration and interpellating that 'people are more worried than ever' because things have got worse, Cooper pledged that 'a Labour Government will bring in stronger border controls to tackle illegal immigration', with proper 'entry and exit checks, so visas can be enforced and criminals stopped'. She went on:

> And we need radical reform when it comes to Europe. To stop the growing crisis at Calais, strengthen restrictions on new countries, change benefit rules so people can't claim when they first arrive, change deportation rules to make it easier to send home EU citizens who commit crimes and to change employment rules to stop employers exploiting cheap migrant labour to undercut wages and jobs. Not free movement, but fair movement.
>
> (Cited in EIN, 2014b)

She insisted that 'it is not racist to be worried about immigration or to want stronger controls', and in an unconvincing attempt to restrict racism to its colour-coded dimension, concluded that 'when a UKIP candidate says [black entertainer] Lenny Henry should leave the country because of the colour of his skin,[13] that is racist. We will never let racism go unchallenged' (cited in EIN, 2014b).

In the toxic climate of racism created in part by the 'really hostile environment' and associated practices, policies and legislation, Farage stated at the 2014 UKIP Conference in September of that year that the issue that would dominate the next election was open door immigration. He added, to a huge cheer of agreement, that we are 'borderless Britain' (cited in *BBC News*, 2014). Racism, particularly xeno-racism was indeed to loom large.[14]

In his speech to the Conservative Party Conference on 2 October 2014, Cameron's mantra was 'A Britain that everyone is proud to call home'. Relating this to controlling immigration, he referred to 'getting our own people fit to work ... controlled borders and an immigration system that puts the British people first'. He went on to interpellate his audience: 'But we know the bigger issue today is migration from within the EU.' Cameron continued with a number of sound bites:

> Immediate access to our welfare system. Paying benefits to families back home. Employment agencies signing people up from overseas and not recruiting here. Numbers that have increased faster than we in this country wanted ... at a level that was too much for our communities, for our labour markets.

Following on from his promise the previous year for a relationship negotiation before a referendum, he declared: 'All of this', he went on, 'has to change – and it will be at the very heart of my renegotiation strategy for Europe'. The interpellation continued: 'Britain, I know you want this sorted so I will go to Brussels, I will not take no for an answer and when it comes to free movement – I will get what Britain needs.' He concluded with a reiteration of his referendum pledge, together with a promise to abolish the UK Human Rights Act enacted by the Labour Party in 1998, and its replacement with a new British Bill of Rights 'rooted in our values' (cited in PoliticsHome, 2014).

As Jonathan Freedland (2014) argued, with respect to the days leading up to the forthcoming general election:

> From now until May, the Tories will seek daily to blunt Ukip's bayonets .... Ukip wants out of the EU, so Cameron promises a referendum. And Ukip slams 'human rights', damned as the co-conspirator of 'political correctness' in sending the country to the dogs, so the Tories promise to crack down on them too – and forget the pesky details.

Freedland concluded that this is 'the pool of fury Ukip drinks from and which the Tories want to channel their way'. It is not about constitutional reform and legal jurisdictions, but an outlet 'for a much more visceral rage, the furious sense that the world is not as it should be – and that someone faraway must be to blame'. Freedland referred to the real problem, not Brussels or the European courts, but the 'borderless forces of globalisation that have upended economic life everywhere' (Freedland, 2014). These forces he failed to name are those of local, regional and international global neoliberal capital, and he did not point out that if Brussels and Strasbourg comprise the distant threat, the racialized 'enemies' on British streets emanate from Sofia and Bucharest.

The 2015 General Election Campaign began officially on 19 December 2014. In addition to the racist consensus that had been forged, the Cameron factor was important in the eventual result of the election. As Deputy Political Editor of the *Telegraph*, Steven Swinford (2015) put it, the Tories had always been acutely aware that Cameron was 'significantly more popular than his own party', whereas the Labour leader was 'afflicted by the opposite problem – Ed Miliband [was] significantly less popular than his party', a factor that was exacerbated by Conservatives questioning Miliband's fitness to lead Britain. The Tories were also remorseless in their attacks on the Liberal Democrats, their Coalition partners of five years, with Cameron repeatedly visiting Liberal Democrat target seats. Finally, while Labour was riven by infighting, Eurosceptic Tory back-benchers were placated by the promise of an EU Referendum. (Swinford, 2015).

Notes

1 Here is not the place to engage with the complex debates pertaining to the cause of the crisis. For opposing views within the Marxist tradition see, for example, Kliman (2015) and Harvey (2015).
2 See Ryder (2014).
3 I say 'right-wing to far right' because although UKIP supremo Farage disassociates himself from far-right politics and racism, many of UKIP's members and supporters do not. The embrace of far-right politics became increasingly the case towards the end of 2018, when a third senior UKIP member left the party over the decision of leader Gerard Batten (who describes Islam as a 'death cult') to appoint the anti-Islam activist Tommy Robinson (real name Stephen Yaxley-Lennon) as an adviser and take the party in a hard-right direction. Yaxley-Lennon is the founder of the far-right English Defence League (EDL), an anti-Muslim street movement
4 Reference to 'non-EU immigrants' relates to the fact that Britain's membership of the European Union at the time allowed free movement of people throughout member states. The main issue, as we shall see, that informed May's determination to exit the EU was a vain attempt to reduce net numbers of immigration, her primary driving force throughout her periods in office.
5 Austerity/immiseration capitalism continues to this day (Butler, 2019; Centre for Cities, 2019; Hill, 2019), despite May's false promise in October 2018 that austerity is over (Kentish, 2018a). In February 2019, the Institute for Fiscal Studies estimated that Chancellor Philip Hammond must find an extra £5 billion in the year's Whitehall spending review to reverse planned cuts and demonstrate that austerity has really ended (following Theresa May, Hammond had claimed that 'austerity is coming to an end' in the Autumn budget of 2018). John McDonnell, the Shadow Chancellor commented: 'The evidence is mounting that, despite …

[the] rhetoric, austerity is not over. Nine years of brutal Tory austerity have wounded our public services and the whole country which relies on them' (Inman, 2019).

6 From a Marxist perspective, capitalism relies for its very existence on the extraction of surplus value from workers who have to sell their labour power to survive: capitalists pay them less than the value they produce, with the value added by workers' labour appropriated as profit by and for the capitalist when goods are sold. This is known as the labour theory of value (LTV). For an elucidation of the LTV, see Marx (1887), especially chapter 1. For a brief summary and a numerical example of how this works, see Cole (2011, pp. 42–44).

7 For an interesting discussion of the origins of the term, 'hostile environment' see *Hansard* (2018).

8 I put 'working class' in brackets because, although the measures pertain to all affected families, the financial requirements clearly discriminate against workers most. From a Marxist perspective, as opposed to a sociological one, the overwhelming majority will be working class because they have to sell their labour power in order to live, irrespective of whether they are middle or working class in its everyday (sociological) sense (see note 6 above).

9 I have changed the tenses of Richmond Chambers' summary from future to present where coherence demands.

10 Interpellation is the *process* by which the legitimation, values, and attitudes required by capitalism are instilled in the populace. Interpellation is the concept neo-Marxist, Louis Althusser (1971, p. 174) used to describe the way in which ruling class ideology is upheld and the class consciousness of the working class – that class's awareness of its structural location in capitalist society – undermined. Interpellation makes us think that ruling class capitalist values are actually congruent with our values as *individuals*.

11 *Border Force* is also the title of a regular documentary about the Force, broadcast on Sky Witness. Here one can see public pedagogies of hatred, contempt and brutality on the front line. One can only surmise what goes on when the cameras aren't running. Television is, of course, and important medium of public pedagogy (e.g. Sandlin *et al.*, 2011, 345–347).

12 The rest of this section of the chapter draws on Cole (2016, pp. 69–70).

13 See *BBC News* (2014).

14 The following analysis draws on Cole (2016, pp. 67–70). Cole (2016, pp. 70–83) includes a timeline of anti-immigrant and racist announcements and events in the seven months leading up the election on 7 May 2015. Two interpellative devices *that continue to this day* were particularly noticeable in the speeches of all the mainstream Westminster politicians prior to that election. They were a constant referral to 'our country', rather than 'the country', and a persistent reference to 'working people'. The former worked to reinforce a sense of verified and demonstrated patriotism as well as a stress on 'us' and 'them' thus excluding 'foreigners', while the latter was useful to the ruling class on at least two levels. First, it served to render social class obsolete (since the term was working people, not the working class); second, it conveyed the message that there are just two groups of people: those who work and those who do not, thus denigrating those unable to find work and people receiving welfare. It also reinforced the myth of the Eastern European worker, who was just in the United Kingdom for benefits and free health and education. If anything was slightly more prominent than racism in the election run-up, it was fears over the demise of the NHS.

2 May ups the ante and becomes Prime Minister

Diane Abbott accuses Theresa May of getting down in the gutter with UKIP.
(Via Twitter, 6 October 2015)

Introduction

In this chapter, I begin by noting that, on winning the 2015 General Election, David Cameron named Theresa May as a possible successor. I move on to an analysis of May's 2015 speech to the Conservative Party Conference, in essence a bid for Conservative Party leadership. In the speech, consistent with her established ideological orientation, May uses public pedagogies of hate and threat, in an attempt to win over the Tory faithful, and to scupper UKIP. I go on to address the 2016 Immigration Act that amounted to 'doubling up' on 'hostile environment' policies. Following the pro-Europe Cameron's resignation in the light of a 'leave' victory in the EU referendum, May's ambition came to fruition and she became Prime Minister. I continue the chapter with a discussion of her offensive against international students, and her relationship with Donald Trump and his world view, which has been critiqued by leading Liberal Democrat, Tim Farron. I go on to address the 8 June 2017 snap General Election, a disastrous and failed attempt to crush all opposition to her. Next, I consider May's pledge to end free movement once and for all, and her 'jump the queue' remark concerning EU nationals. I conclude the chapter with an evaluation of the 2018 White Paper on Immigration that has been described as the biggest single attack on migrant rights in a generation.

Prime Minister Cameron names May as a possible successor

On 7 May 2015, the Conservatives won an outright majority in the General Election. In March of that year, David Cameron had said he would not serve a third term as prime minister if the Conservatives were to remain in power after the election, amid growing speculation among Conservative MPs that he might, in fact, quit after the EU Referendum (Grice, 2015), before the end of the 2020 third term. As he put it:

> There definitely comes a time where a fresh pair of eyes and fresh leadership would be good, and the Conservative Party has got some great people coming up – the *Theresa Mays*, and the George Osbornes, and the Boris Johnsons. There's plenty of talent there. I'm surrounded by very good people.
>
> (Cited in Grice, 2015; emphasis added)

As Andrew Grice (2015) has argued, speaking about possible departure dates is a minefield that impacted on both Margaret Thatcher, who had stated that she intended to 'go on and on', and was subsequently ousted by her party, and Tony Blair, who ruled out a fourth term, and came under intense (successful) pressure to stand down a year earlier than he had intended.

May's bid for the Conservative Party leadership

No doubt cognisant of this potential opportunity for self-advancement on 6 October, Home Secretary Theresa May made a speech to the 2015 Conservative Party Conference, widely viewed as a bid for Conservative leadership. Thus, the then Shadow Secretary of State for International Development, Diane Abbott tweeted: 'Theresa May gets down in the gutter with UKIP chasing votes for her leadership bid', while Steven Woolfe MEP, and at the time UKIP Immigration Spokesman (*sic*), declared, also on Twitter: 'Theresa May's speech on migration today is simply posturing to the Tory faithful, to prop herself up for a leadership bid in 2020' (cited in Dearden, 2015).

A leadership bid was also transparent for the then Executive Editor, Politics, James Kirkup at the Tory-supporting online 'broadsheet', the *Telegraph*. As he stated, 'It's hard to know where to start with Theresa May's awful, ugly, misleading, cynical and irresponsible speech to the Conservative Party conference today':

> If you haven't seen reports of it, allow me to summarise: 'Immigrants are stealing your job, making you poorer and ruining your country. Never mind the facts, just feel angry at foreigners. And make me Conservative leader.'
>
> (Kirkup, 2015)

Kirkup analysed two of May's key sentences as follows:

1   *And we know that for people in low-paid jobs, wages are forced down even further while some people are forced out of work altogether.*
    He pointed out that a review of the evidence by May's own officials concluded: 'There is relatively little evidence that migration has caused statistically significant displacement of UK natives from the labour market in periods when the economy is strong' (see Devlin *et al.*, 2014).
2   Immigration makes it *impossible to build a cohesive society.*
    As Kirkup rightly replied, this is more of a subjective issue. However, he reminded his readers that there is (considerable) 'evidence [...] that the less personal acquaintance with migrants a person has, the more worried they are about immigration'. As he went on, *if* immigration makes UK society less cohesive, that may be partly the result of 'politicians pandering to ignorance and prejudice and wilfully distorting the evidence to persuade people to be angry and afraid' (Kirkup, 2015). Kirkup concluded his comments on this particular public pedagogy of hate in her speech:

> The Home Secretary says she's worried about immigration social cohesion. If she really wants to help, she could start by abandoning this cheap and nasty speech and the politics behind it. [...] But then [...] political ambition is more important than talking responsibly and honestly about immigration, isn't it? What a curious form of leadership.

In her speech, May yet again blamed immigrants for pressures on public services: 'It's difficult for schools and hospitals and core infrastructure like housing and transport to cope' (Stone, 2016), whereas the real blame should be attributed to a Conservative government that refuses to properly fund the NHS, which it continues to privatize by the back door (Forster, 2017), and prioritized at the time new grammar schools over more schools for all (schools nationwide are set to lose £3 billion a year in real terms by 2020; see Pearce, 2017), and refused to build affordable housing.

Referring specifically to asylum seekers, May suggested that they should not even be allowed into Britain before their claims were assessed:

> At the moment, the main way people claim asylum here is when they're already in Britain. That fails on three counts ... I want to offer asylum and refuge to people in parts of the world affected by conflict and oppression, rather than to those who have made it to Britain.
>
> (Cited in Stone, 2016)

Refugee Council chief executive Maurice Wren responded to May's disturbing public pedagogy of threat as follows:

> The Home Secretary's clear intention to close Britain's border to refugees fleeing for their lives is thoroughly chilling, as is her bitter attack on the fundamental principle enshrined in international law that people fleeing persecution should be able to claim asylum in Britain.
>
> (Cited in Stone, 2016)

In addition, May reinforced her public pedagogy of hate, this time labelling those seeking sanctuary as lawbreakers who contribute nothing to the economy, claiming that a significant number of asylum seekers are 'foreign criminals', and, contrary to the vast majority of economists' analyses, summed up her view that 'the net economic and fiscal effect of high immigration is close to zero' (cited in Stone, 2016).

Britain is and has always been a multicultural society (Cole, 2018b, 99–100; see also Fryer, 1984; Visram, 1986; Walvin, 1973). May, however, dismissed the idea that Britain was a 'country of immigrants', claiming that 'we have until recently always been a country of remarkable population stability' (cited in Stone, 2016).

The 2016 Immigration Act

On 12 May 2016, the Immigration Act that focuses on 'illegal migration' and accompanying punitive measures, came into force. Like other facets of the 'really hostile environment', the Act will impact on all migrants. Its key changes are:

- Employers who hire illegal migrants and the workers themselves face criminal sanctions.
- Migrants who do not have permission to be in the UK can have certain privileges revoked, such as the seizure of their driving licence and the freezing of their bank accounts.
- It becomes a criminal offence for a landlord to knowingly rent premises to an illegal migrant, with up to five years in prison for offenders.
- The 'deport first, appeal later' scheme becomes extended to all migrants.
- Pregnant women can now only be detained by immigration authorities for up to 72 hours (or one week with special permission).
- Arrangements are now to be made to relocate unaccompanied refugee children from other countries in Europe to the UK (Lea, 2016).

The Joint Council for the Welfare of Immigrants (JCWI) (2016) welcomed the 72 hour limit for pregnant women, the relocation of child refugees, and another feature of the Act – immigration detainees not facing deportation after a criminal conviction are now entitled to an automatic bail hearing after four months of detention. These were all achieved, it points out, through months of hard work by campaigners, NGOs and a number of parliamentarians. With respect to other features of the Act, it offered the following overall critique:

> these concessions do little to ameliorate the full force of the measures brought in by this Act which will make the UK a more hostile and unwelcoming place. The ... Act ... introduces a vast number of draconian, unaccountable and poorly thought out powers and offences that will have a huge impact on the lives of both migrants and British citizens, particularly those in black and minority ethnic communities. It sets back the progress of integration, and many of the measures that the Government claims are to protect migrants from exploitation, actually increase the risk of this.
>
> (JCWI, 2016)

'This doubling down on "hostile environment" policies', it continues, can be seen in the following changes brought in by the Act. Here are some of the main problems, as identified by the JCWI:

Labour market exploitation

- Given that prosecutors can confiscate anything acquired through 'illegal working', this can lead to further exploitation since unscrupulous employers can threaten to report people for this new 'crime'.

Driving licences, bank accounts and powers of immigration officials

- The Act introduces new stop and search powers where police have 'reasonable grounds' for believing that someone is not lawfully resident in the UK and is in possession of a driving licence. Given the history of discrimination in the use of 'stop and search' in the UK it is very hard to see how this power will not result in black and minority ethnic drivers being targeted by immigration officials or the police.
- With respect to freezing bank accounts, given the long record of poor decision-making by the Home Office, this is likely to impact on many people who have every right to be here. It also increases the risk of exploitation of undocumented migrants, as they will be driven to use

cash, lodge money with others and use black market financial services.

- More generally, the Act gives immigration officials new powers to search property and seize documents, as well as to perform strip searches of individuals in order to search for documents.

Landlord immigration checks

- As far as these checks are concerned, the JCWI has found that this scheme is unworkable; that it causes discrimination against those who aren't British; and it has a disproportionate effect on members of minority ethnic communities. Landlords faced with a potential fine or prison may take the safe option and rent to those with a British passport where possible. Furthermore, the Home Secretary is granted the power to require a landlord to evict tenants who do not have a 'right to rent' from their property, by issuing a written notice, for which there is no judicial oversight.

Finally, out-of-country appeals, up to the passing of the Act were restricted to foreign national offenders, but now apply across the board. It is far more difficult to appeal from abroad for a number of reasons, including the cost and the difficulty of gathering evidence and presenting a case when not physically present (JCWI, 2016) (see Note 1, in Introduction to this book).

'Leave' side wins the referendum and May replaces Cameron as Prime Minister

The Referendum to decide whether the UK should stay in or leave the European Union was held on 23 June 2016, following a four-month campaign, with Theresa May and David Cameron joining the Remain camp. Satnam Virdee and Brendan McGeever (2017) identify the two distinct organizational formations behind the Leave campaign: the official Leave campaign, Vote Leave, composed of right-wing Conservatives, notably Boris Johnson, as well as lone UKIP MP, Douglas Carswell, a couple of Labour MPs and Independent, Frank Field; and the UKIP-led project, Leave.EU, funded by multi-millionaires Aaron Banks and Richard Tice, and fronted by Farage.

When pro-EU membership leaflets costing £9m of public money were sent to 27 million UK homes in early April, Farage declared it 'outrageous' to spend taxpayers' money 'to tell us how we should think and how we should vote'. Cameron stressed the government was 'not neutral' in the referendum and the cost was 'money well spent' (Webber, 2016).

From the Leave side, there were racist scare stories about how soon Turkey might be able to join the EU, while one of the most surreal scenes in the campaign witnessed Farage and Bob Geldof, co-founder of Band Aid, throw insults at each other in a mock 'nautical battle', as Farage led a flotilla of fishing boats up the Thames to urge Parliament to take back control of British waters. As Esther Webber (2016) puts it, 'His Brexit armada was greeted by a rival Remain fleet carrying Mr Geldof, who yelled that the UKIP leader was "no fisherman's friend"', while Farage 'accused Mr Geldof of "mocking" impoverished fishermen'. Shortly afterwards, Farage released an infamous poster bearing the words 'breaking point', depicting a line of migrants at the Slovenia border (Webber, 2016).

Significantly, coverage of immigration more than tripled over the course of the campaign, rising faster than any other political issue (Moore and Ramsay, 2017). Michael Moore and Gordon Ramsay summarize the results of their survey of the coverage in all articles published about the 2016 EU referendum by the leading UK national news outlets online, including national press, digital-only news services, and the online news services of the leading broadcasters for the period of the official referendum campaign (2017, 2):

- Immigration was the most prominent referendum issue, based on the number of times it led newspaper print front pages (there were 99 front pages about immigration, 82 about the economy).
- Coverage of the effects of immigration was overwhelmingly negative. Migrants were blamed for many of Britain's economic and social problems – most notably for putting unsustainable pressure on public services.
- Specific nationalities were singled out for particularly negative coverage – especially Turks and Albanians, but also Romanians and Poles.
- The majority of negative coverage of specific foreign nationals was published by three news sites: the *Express*, the *Daily Mail*, and the *Sun*.

(Moore and Ramsay, 2017, 8–9)

These findings serve to underline the Islamophobic and xeno-racist nature of the reporting, and serve to detract from Corbyn's state of inequality in the UK agenda.

The result of the Referendum was an unexpected win by Leave of 51.9 per cent to Remain's 48.1 per cent. With respect to social class and age, while exit polls showed that around two-thirds of those who voted in social classes D and E chose Leave (Ashcroft, 2016), it should also be pointed out that the proportion of Leave voters who were of the lowest two social classes was just 24 per cent (Dorling, 2016). As Satnam Virdee and Brendan McGeever (2017) point out, Leave voters among the elite and middle classes were crucial to the final outcome, with almost three in five votes coming from those in social classes A, B and C1 (Dorling, 2016). Additionally, age seems to have been central to the Brexit vote since, while 62 per cent of 25–34-year-olds chose to Remain, 60 per cent of those aged 65 and over voted to Leave (Virdee and McGeever, 2017). 'In sum', they conclude,

> it is too simplistic to suggest that Brexit constituted the revolt of the 'left behind'; rather, what needs to be understood is how the campaign to Leave managed to successfully cohere a significant cross-class coalition of middle-aged and older men and women.
>
> (Virdee and McGeever, 2017)

The 'left behind' that they are referring to are those of pension age, low-skilled and less-educated blue-collar workers, and others pushed to the margins by neoliberalism, the same constituency that had voted UKIP in the 2014 European Parliamentary elections (Virdee and McGeever, 2017).

The day after the Brexit result, Cameron, having staked his position on a Remain vote, announced that he would resign, admitting that the country now needed 'fresh leadership', that is 'strong, determined and committed' (Wright, 2016).

After receiving the overwhelming support of Tory MPs in the ensuing Tory Leadership contest, Theresa May stated:

> I am pleased with this result, and very grateful to my colleagues for their support. There is a big job before us: to unite our party and the country, to negotiate the best possible deal as we leave the EU, and to make Britain work for everyone. I am the only candidate capable of delivering these three things as prime minister, and … it is clear that I am also the only one capable of drawing support from the whole of the Conservative Party.
>
> (Cited in Boyle *et al.*, 2016)

The vacuous nature of these claims would come back to haunt her as she quickly began to preside over a totally disunited party, a divided country, and a deal that she was unable to get through parliament.

When the last remaining candidate withdrew from the leadership race on 11 July, precluding the need for a vote by Tory Party members, May was confirmed as Conservative Party leader. Cameron resigned as Prime

Minister two days later, and May became Britain's second female Prime Minister. In her post-Brexit prime ministerial statement, focusing on 'fighting against burning injustice', she said she wanted to address the 'ordinary working-class family' and that her government would be driven by their interests, not those of the privileged few (GOV.UK, 2016). Despite mentioning black people in this pledge (shallow words in the light of the Windrush scandal (see pp. 76–82 of this book), her failure to mention (potential) immigrants and asylum seekers, given how May's 'hostile environment' was directed at them, was no doubt an intentional omission. Unsurprisingly, given her *real* position on the political spectrum, her first appointments tilted the cabinet to the right (Stewart, 2016).

Theresa May's premiership, 2016–2019: the 'really hostile environment' continues with a vengeance

Kick out international students

Shortly after May became Prime Minister, she returned to her familiar theme of reducing net migration to the tens of thousands. As it was reported in the *Independent*, May believed that further tough regulation on universities by scrutinising foreign students' visas was a way of doing this, since she believed that higher education institutions had become an easy route into Britain for economic migrants. In a confidential letter to other ministers, she also argued that universities should 'develop sustainable funding models that are not so dependent on international students' (Yeung, 2016).

Peter Yeung (2016) also reported that Theresa May could have wrongly deported tens of thousands of international students, with the Upper Tribunal (Asylum and Immigration) ruling that the then Home Secretary's evidence suffered from 'multiple frailties and shortcomings' (cited in Yeung, 2016). The students were accused of cheating in English language tests in 2014, with May, acting swiftly to cancel, cut short, or refuse, the visas of 35,870 students who had taken the test (Merrick, 2019). In February 2019, it was revealed that some of these students were still being detained and are living in 'terror', with some in poverty or having mental health problems (Merrick, 2019). Labour MP, Stephen Timms said ministers must allow the students to sit a fresh test, grant visas to those who pass and allow them 'time to complete their studies and to clear their names' (cited in Merrick, 2019).

Theresa May refuses to roll back 'hostile environment' policy

Farron lays into May

In late January 2017, Theresa May visited the new US president Donald J. Trump in Washington. Criticising this visit a few months later at his Liberal Democratic Party's Conference, Tim Farron laid into Theresa May who he noted 'took office claiming she would be a social justice crusader. And here she is today, to the right of Thatcher, holding hands with Donald Trump' (cited in Lindsay, 2017).[1]

May's government, he went on, is 'a government that is as anti-refugees as Nigel Farage'. 'One of the most despicable things this Government has done', he suggested, 'happened quietly, in a ministerial written statement on the day that Article 50 passed the House of Commons', when the 'Home Office quietly confirmed that Britain would stop taking in desperate, unaccompanied child refugees.' This was not 'because the crisis was at an end or because we had rescued the thousands of children that the Government had promised, under duress, to help', he continued. 'Of the tens of thousands of unaccompanied children fleeing war and destitution, in the end we will take just 350.' The reason was 'because they calculated that they could get away with it'. 'But just to make sure', he concludes, 'they sneaked out the news on the same day that Tory and Labour MPs voted Article 50 through. A despicable act, done in a despicable way'.[2]

The 8 June snap General Election

On 18 April 2017, May announced a snap General Election to take place on 8 June, giving as her reason that the opposition parties were jeopardising her government's preparations for Brexit (the departure of the UK from the EU) (Asthana *et al.*, 2017). It was a drastic miscalculation for May that changed parliamentary arithmetic from a Tory working majority of 17 to a hung parliament, forcing May to enter a 'confidence and supply' agreement with the Democratic Unionist Party (DUP) (the DUP agrees to back the Conservatives on key votes in return for political favours).

Described by Scottish Nationalist Party (SNP) leader, Nicola Sturgeon as a naked power grab and a bid to crush all opposition (Hunt and Wheeler, 2017), the catastrophic changes in May's fortunes can be viewed as the result of a number of factors. These include actually calling the election when she had previously ruled it out; running a presidential-type campaign when she doesn't like media interviews and dodges TV debates and big rallies; and constantly repeating 'strong and stable', while underestimating and not taking seriously opposition leader Jeremy Corbyn and his anti-austerity message (Hunt and Wheeler, 2017). For insiders, according to Hunt and Wheeler (2017), the turning point in the campaign was May's u-turn on social care. Team May had apparently been so confident of victory that it felt bold enough to cost-cut. Thus there were proposals for a 'dementia tax' that would lead to more people having to sell their homes to pay for care; for means testing the winter fuel allowance (an annual tax-free payment for those in receipt of state pension) and for ending the 'triple lock' that guarantees a minimum 2.5 per cent annual increase in state pension. Finally, May was an introvert by Westminster standards (towards the end of the campaign she had to rely on Boris Johnson to whip up the crowds) conducting a negative and uninspiring campaign (Hunt and Wheeler, 2017).

Tens of thousands and the end of free movement

On Friday, 2 June 2017, political journalist, Ashley Cowburn (2017) reported that May had stated at a campaign rally the day before that she 'would be working' to achieve the 'tens of thousands' target, pledged ad finitum and ad nauseum, and repeated in the Conservative Manifesto, published in May 2017, by 2022 (Cowburn, 2017). According to an editorial run by the former Chancellor George Osborne, Editor of the *London Evening Standard*, none of the senior members of the Cabinet supported the pledge privately and said retaining it was 'economically illiterate' (cited in Cowburn, 2017).

May's claims as to the negative effects of immigration were subsequently repeated again in Prime Minister's Questions in September 2017 (Hughes, 2017), while in that same month, Liberal Democratic Leader, Vince Cable claimed that while he was Business Secretary in the ConDem Government and May was Home Secretary, she suppressed up to nine reports showing no immigration impact on jobs and (contrary to the imperatives of capitalism) on wages because the findings were 'inconvenient' to the government, a claim denied by a spokesperson for the Prime Minister (Casalicchio, 2017).

On his BBC1 programme on the eve of the 2018 Tory Party Conference on 30 September, Andrew Marr interviewed Theresa May on a number of issues that included her 'hostile environment' and the Immigration Act of 2014. She apologized for their combined effects on the Windrush generation (see Chapter 4 for a discussion of this scandal) that Marr described as a 'burning injustice' (a reference to her 2016 prime ministerial victory statement). However, after being asked repeatedly by Marr to apologize for the 'hostile environment' policy itself and the accompanying Act, May refused to apologize for either, and managed to slip in: 'we maintain the compliant environment policy' (changing 'really hostile' to 'compliant' was announced by Sajid Javid when he became Home Secretary in March 2018).

At the conference itself, May reiterated her 'end of free movement' pledge and her promise to reduce net migration, but without a mention of actual numbers:

> And with control of our borders, we can do something that no British government has been able to do in decades – restore full and complete control of who comes into this country to the democratically elected representatives of the British people.... The free movement of people will end, once and for all.... Those with the skills we need, who want to come here and work hard, will find a welcome. But we will be able to reduce the numbers, as we promised.
>
> (Cited in Whitfield, 2018)

However, asked during Prime Minister's Questions on 9 December 2018 if the government still wanted to keep immigration in the tens of thousands, May simply said 'yes'.

EU nationals 'jump the queue': May plays the (xeno-) 'race' card

In November 2018, May faced a backlash (*BBC News*, 2018a) over remarks made in a speech to business leaders, in which she again vowed to end EU free movement once and for all after Brexit. May stated in a bid possibly aimed at promoting xeno-racism Europe-wide, rather than Eastern Europe specific:

> It will no longer be the case that EU nationals, regardless of the skills or experience they have to offer, can jump the queue ahead of engineers from Sydney or software developers from Delhi.
>
> (Cited in *BBC News*, 2018a)

The European Parliament's Brexit co-ordinator Guy Verhofstadt responded, 'EU citizens living, working, contributing to UK communities, didn't "jump the queue" and neither did UK nationals in Europe', since they 'were exercising rights which provided freedom and opportunities'. He went on to say: 'We will fight to ensure these continue in the future, especially after any transition' (cited in *BBC News*, 2018a). Meanwhile, EU citizens living in the UK took to social media to accuse the Prime

Minister of using them as scapegoats to shore up support for her Brexit agreement (*BBC News*, 2018a).

Writing for the *Huffington Post*, Tanja Bueltmann, pro-vice-chancellor and a history professor at Northumbria University, underlined the effects of May's ongoing public pedagogy of hate:

> May's words ... are not only insulting, but also directly harmful. They continue to invoke the lies that EU citizens here have not contributed. It is in such rhetoric that we can find the roots of hate against us. This hate can manifest in verbal abuse – from telling us to 'f*** off back to the s***hole' we came from to labelling us 'enemy aliens'.
>
> (Cited in Kentish, 2018b)

She went on,

> Home Office figures clearly show a rise in hate crimes against EU citizens, and police already predict another rise as Brexit day comes closer. The EU referendum, and everything May and her government have done since then, directly enabled this.
>
> (Cited in Kentish, 2018b)

Bueltmann concluded by accusing May of 'pinning people against people, casting one group as better than another', adding,

> That is despicable. And it is one of the hallmarks of xenophobia [I would say, 'xeno-racism']. As a result, there can now be no doubt that EU citizens need to brace themselves for yet more hate over the coming months.
>
> (Cited in Kentish, 2018b)

May was challenged by an SNP MP, Philippa Whitford in the House of Commons over the comment, who asked if she would apologize for managing 'to insult and upset over 3 million European citizens who live and work in this country.' May replied, 'I should not have used that language in that speech' (Holton and Smout, 2018).

The 2018 White Paper on immigration

Free Movement (2018) has provided a useful summary and critique of the 2018 White Paper on immigration that it describes as a 'charter for the wealthy'. The organization, which offers updates, commentary and advice on immigration and asylum law, argues that there is one, overwhelming message in the document: 'prioritise and facilitate movement for those with access to large sums of capital; and the ongoing importance of a migrant's country of origin in line with political expediency'. 'In short', while it claims that its aim is to 'attract the brightest and best to a United Kingdom that is open for business', the reality is that it will 'attract the richest migrants, highest earners and create parallel rules for numerous types of migrants, dependent upon the trade deals struck in a post-Brexit world' (Free Movement, 2018). It notes that the White Paper does not propose any immigration rule changes, but that these will be published following a year of 'extensive engagement'.

The White Paper's key message is that, post-Brexit, 'Everyone will be required to obtain a permission if they want to come to the UK and to work or study here', but that until the end of the implementation period, EU free movement rules will continue to apply. From 1 January 2021, EU citizens and their family members must apply under the EU Settlement Scheme, and will have until June 2021 to do so (Free Movement, 2018).

The White Paper allows low-skilled migrants to come to the UK to work for up to a year in, for example, skill gap areas such as 'sectors like construction and social care'. This route will contain a 12-month cooling-off period to prevent further applications for leave from such migrants. Most importantly, the Immigration Law Practitioners Association (ILPA), a group of leading immigration law practitioners that promotes and improves the advising and representation of immigrants, notes that 'the visa ... will not carry entitlements to access public funds or rights to extend a stay, switch to other routes, bring dependants or lead to permanent settlement' (cited in Free Movement, 2018). As Free Movement (2018) argues, this 'is particularly perverse, as it is assumed that low-skilled migrants do not pay taxation'. In fact, migrants on work-based visas all pay tax on their UK earnings. It is therefore unclear as to the policy reason for denying people who pay for public services through general taxation the right to then access those self-same public services that are paid for through general taxation (Free Movement, 2018).

There is also a salary requirement of £30,000 (or the 25 per cent earnings threshold of that occupation, whichever is higher) for skilled migrants seeking five-year visas. Free Movement (2018) points out that the current 25 per cent salary threshold for qualified teachers in primary and secondary schools is £22,022, and for nurses, the minimum salary does not reach £30,000 until they are at band 7: typically a specialist nurse in a particular area of medicine, or a ward manager with budgetary control and responsibility for management of the ward's nursing staff. The £30,000 threshold will, therefore, mean an incapability of responding to shortages in primary and secondary teaching and nursing at the junior end (Free Movement,

2018). This means that 'the government has chosen to completely ignore the contributions that key public sector employees, such as nurses and teachers, make to the UK economy' (Free Movement, 2018).

The White Paper refers to 'low-risk' countries from which migrants can apply for a visa-free Electronic Travel Authority that will allow them to apply to enter the country without the need for documentary leave to enter/ remain for six months. This serves political expediency and reinforces detrimental structural stereotypes about certain cohorts of migrants. The ILPA notes that it is unclear why some countries are classified as 'low-risk' while others are not.

Commenting on the White Paper, Ed Lewis, migration campaigner at Global Justice Now, reminds us that 'The Brexit result did not require an end to free movement – this is a political choice by the most anti-migrant prime minister in living memory' (Global Justice Now, 2018). As he puts it:

> The white paper is the biggest single attack on rights we've seen in a generation. It will create 'Fortress Britain' where migrants come and go at the behest of big business but lack many of the rights which EU migrants have enjoyed to date. It is a recipe for a race to the bottom in terms of worker pay and conditions. As a country that pillaged and exploited the world to gain its wealth – and still does today – it is unconscionable to further close our doors to human beings.
>
> (Cited in Global Justice Now, 2018)

Lewis goes on, 'If people are worried about having their wages undercut by migrants, the white paper makes this more likely. You can only avoid this when you give migrants real rights. The white paper is all about removing rights' (cited in Global Justice Now, 2018). 'Perhaps the most shocking aspect of the White Paper', he argues, 'is that it wants Britain to sign up to dodgy deals with repressive regimes like Turkey or Egypt in the hope those countries will keep refugees and migrants out of Britain' (cited in Global Justice Now, 2018). Such a policy has resulted in thousands of deaths in the Mediterranean and 'slave camps in Libya'. 'On top of this', Lewis points out, 'the government wants to sign up to a version of the Dublin Convention which leaves migrants in already struggling countries like Italy and Greece': 'This is truly a charter for making our human rights responsibilities "someone else's problem"' (cited in Global Justice Now, 2018). He then makes links to the source of migrants' needs to migrate:

> Britain is a country that continues to derive much wealth off the backs of other countries around the world. Too often, people are here

because of the effects of wars, arms sales, trade deals, tax avoidance and corporate behaviour sanctioned by Britain. It is outrageous to drain other countries of wealth and then refuse to give a place to those who lose out from these policies.

(Cited in Global Justice Now, 2018)

'The freedom to move', Lewis concludes, 'shouldn't just be confined to the rich or middle classes' (cited in Global Justice Now, 2018). The case for a borderless socialist future is made in Chapter 5 of this book.

Notes

1 To be fair, it should be pointed out that the gesture was apparently nothing to do with close affection between the pair – but instead Trump was leaning on May while suffering a phobic episode. He is said to be scared of germs – but his fear of stairs and ramps is even worse, and is known as 'bathmophobia'. A White House spokesperson stated: 'He hates heights where you can see the ground or sharp inclines even more than germs. He particularly dislikes staircases and his biggest nightmare of all is a dirty stair rail' (cited in Campbell, 2017). If this is the case, one would have thought he could have held May's arm rather than her hand.

2 Farron's speech, which was patriotic and anti-socialist ('capitalism versus socialism, has been overtaken by a new debate about the sort of country we are'), is also discussed in the Introduction to this book (see pp. 5–6).

3   The hostile environment: general impact

> We will do everything we can to make sure that you are often not success-ful [in claiming asylum].
>
> (Sajid Javid, reported in the *Guardian*, 2 January 2019)

Introduction

I begin Chapter 3 of the book with some snapshots of the 'really hostile environment' in action – in health and education. I go on to consider its overall impact on asylum seekers, with respect to accommodation, the right to work, detention, and what happens if refugee status is granted. I then address the effect of the hostile environment on asylum seekers who are victims of torture, before looking at the issues surrounding migrants trying to cross the English Channel, and Home Secretary, Sajid Javid's response to this. I end the section on asylum seekers with a consideration of health care. I conclude the chapter with an analysis of the specific impact of the 'really hostile environment' on women, with respect to both detention and domestic violence. As concerns the latter, I include a critical analysis of the Domestic Violence and Abuse Bill.

The 'really hostile environment' in action: some snapshots

Health

According to former head of NHS Digital, Kingsley Manning, he repeat-edly clashed with Theresa May's Home Office over requests to hand over confidential patient data to help trace 'immigration offenders' (Travis, 2017a). He said he was 'under immense pressure' to share patient data despite concerns about the legal basis and fears it would undermine claims that NHS Digital was 'a safe haven' for personal data (Travis, 2017a). According to Alan Travis, then Home Affairs editor for the *Guardian*, writing in early 2017, 'the non-clinical personal details including last known address, GP's details and date registered with their doctor, of more than 8,100 people ... [over the previous year were] ... passed to Home Office immigration enforcement'. When Manning first got the job in 2013, the year after May had named the 'really hostile environment', he asked the Home Office what the legal basis was for handing over such data, and was told that the 'Home Office view was that tracing illegal immigrants was a manifesto commitment'. If he didn't 'agree to cooperate [with the sharing of patient data] they would simply take the issue to Downing Street' (Travis, 2017a).

Also writing for the *Guardian*, this is how freelance feature writer, Simon Usborne (2018) begins his survey of how the hostile environment has crept into everyday life in the UK.

> For a doctor in Birmingham, it was the pregnant patient eating less to save money to cover an NHS bill. For a primary school teacher in an inner-city school, it was the moment he sat down with new parents for an uncomfortable conversation about their child's nationality. For a London lecturer, it was the worry that A-level students were being put off university for fear of being deported. In banks, hospitals, lettings agencies, schools and lecture theatres, the government's current immigration policy has effectively erected a border within, along which people delivering vital services are coming to terms with unwanted new powers.

NHS doctor Neal Russell (2018) refers to a political agenda that 'has been allowed to stand in the way of patients accessing healthcare'. He goes on to explain that the effects of the government's 'really hostile environment' towards migrants in the NHS became clear to him when, as a children's doctor, he saw a new born baby girl become one of its victims. Her mother, he points out, was an undocumented migrant living in the UK, who had attended an appointment during pregnancy, but was deterred from coming back for further care because of the cost, which for maternity care for migrants starts at £4,000 (apparently a mark-up of 150 per cent of the actual cost) and can rise to tens of thousands for more complex care (Russell, 2018). Many women, Russell (2018) points out, have been sent intimidating letters, while pregnant, 'threatening Home Office intervention if bills were unpaid'. After delivery, moreover, they are even subjected to court proceedings. Understandably, he continues, the woman I treated avoided antenatal care after that first encounter, but at the last minute, as she started her contractions, fear for her baby meant that she did go to hospital. She gave birth to a baby who had complications with permanent implications (Russell, 2018).

Episodes like this, Russell (2018) points out, 'are recorded as involving women with "social issues", who have "poor engagement with antenatal care" ', with those who cannot pay being referred to the Home Office for potential detention and deportation. Given that the NHS 'has abandoned its founding principles in service of a political agenda', Russell and his colleagues are handing back medals given to them by the UK Government for humanitarian work on Ebola in West Africa (Russell, 2018).

Chaminda Jayanetti (2018) tells a similar story, with hundreds of patients being denied treatment for serious health problems including cancer, arrhythmia and cardiac chest pains. In one case, a patient with advanced stage cancer died after she went a year without treatment because an NHS hospital demanded £30,000 upfront to provide chemotherapy (Jayanetti, 2018).

Data obtained by the *Guardian* under the Freedom of Information (FOI) Act showed that across 84 of England's 148 acute hospital trusts, 2,279 patients were charged upfront between October 2017 and June 2018. Of these, 341 patients in 61 trusts did not proceed with their intended treatments or appointments after being told to pay (Jayanetti, 2018). As Jayanetti (2018) points out, the true figure is certain to be higher, since 64 trusts did not provide figures.

Labour's Shadow Health Secretary, Jon Ashworth, called for upfront charging to be suspended:

> Patients feeling they have no option but to deny themselves treatment because of Theresa May's obnoxious 'hostile environment' agenda is not only leaving people who are ill without help but could potentially have wider public health implication as well.
>
> (Cited in Jayanetti, 2018)

The FOI data revealed that across 80 hospital trusts, the total amount charged upfront to patients – including most of those who did not proceed with treatment – was about £4m for the first eight months of the upfront charging regimen that came into effect in October 2017 (Jayanetti, 2018).

Education

With respect to the education system, Sally Weale (2018a), education correspondent for the *Guardian*, has pointed out how headteachers and campaigners have expressed outrage at the fact that pupils who are among the poorest in society are missing out on free school meals because their parents/carers have no access to benefits as a part of the rule introduced in 2012 known as 'no recourse to public funds' (NRPF). As Weale (2018a) explains, all children in reception, year 1 and year 2 automatically get free meals, irrespective of immigration status, and refugees are entitled to free meals. However, older children whose parents'/carers' access to benefits is limited by the NRPF condition are being denied free meals, though many say they lack the means to pay.

According to The Children's Society (2016), over a two-year period more than 50,000 individuals with dependents had the 'no recourse to public funds' condition applied to their leave to remain. Its chief executive, Matthew Reed commented:

> It is shocking to think of any child going hungry at school, but the reality is that there are thousands of children in the UK living in families who are facing destitution but being denied vital benefits like free school meals – all because of their immigration status.
>
> (Cited in The Children's Society, 2016)

Usborne (2018) cites academic, Francesca Zanatta, a lecturer in children's rights at the University of East London, a university that, along with all other UK universities, is legally required to perform immigration checks on behalf of the government. Zanatta argues that the 'really hostile environment', of which she is now a part, 'is like a disease, a virus', that she sees 'as an infringement of the universal declaration of human rights which says everyone has a right to education' (cited in Usborne, 2018). As we have seen, international students have been targeted by May to drive down net migration. Many such students have to take 'credibility interviews' to make sure they are 'genuine students'.

Zanatta points out that, while lecturers do not perform the checks themselves, staff feel uncomfortable with the environment created by them. She also fears the effects on some UK students:

> Recently, I was approached by a secondary school student whose friend didn't really have ID because they had arrived here aged three. They asked what would I recommend. And I didn't have an answer.... People are very fearful of exposing themselves to the possibility of being deported.
>
> (Cited in Usborne, 2018)

Moreover, students from some countries staying longer than six months must register with the police within a week of arriving. Currently (GOV.

UK, 2019) this comprises some 40 countries, of which over 60 per cent are predominantly Muslim countries. Universities must also subject international students to more rigorous attendance rules and periodic document checks (Usborne, 2018). Failure to comply (Maisuria and Cole, 2017) can result in the loss of the licence that allows institutions to admit international students, whose fees they increasingly rely on to balance their books (Usborne, 2018).

Impact on asylum seekers

On 1 March 2017 a the *Guardian* investigation (Lyons *et al.*, 2017) reported that 'Britain is one of the worst destinations for people seeking asylum in western Europe', taking fewer refugees; offering less generous financial support; providing housing that is often sub-standard; and not giving asylum seekers the right to work. Reflecting the hostile environment, Alex Fraser, director of refugee support at the British Red Cross, stated: 'I don't think we will see a reduction … by making the experience tougher. All it will do is make the experience of people in the system more difficult' (cited in Lyons *et al.*, 2017).

Accommodation

With respect to accommodation for asylum seekers, on 31 January, Travis (2017b) described a House of Commons Home Affairs Select Committee report that exposed how some destitute asylum seekers are housed in accommodation infested with mice, rats and bedbugs, with one woman complaining of a kitchen 'full of mice' that 'ran across the dining room table' while they were eating, and a torture survivor for whom the presence and noise of rats triggered flashbacks to the rat-infested cell where he had been detained and tortured (Travis, 2017b). Moreover, asylum seeker housing tends to be concentrated in the most deprived areas: the report noted that while there were 1,042 asylum seekers housed in Bolton and 1,029 in Rochdale, there were only 88 housed in the then Home Secretary, Amber Rudd's[1] Hastings and Rye constituency and none at all in Theresa May's Maidenhead constituency (Travis, 2017b). Committee chair Yvette Cooper said that the state of accommodation was a 'disgrace', with 'lack of healthcare for pregnant women, or inadequate support for victims of rape and torture' (cited in Travis, 2017b).

The right to work

As far as the right to work is concerned, in a parliamentary debate, Sarah Newton, a parliamentary undersecretary of state at the Home Office, stated in a distinctive Tory callous fashion, typical of the 'really hostile environment', that the government opposed giving asylum seekers the right to work in order to ensure 'that access to jobs is prioritised for British citizens and those with leave to remain' and to avoid a 'pull factor' for asylum seekers (cited in Lyons *et al.*, 2017).

Detention

As Niamh McIntyre and Diane Taylor (2018) explain, immigrants can be detained at any time and those who do not speak English and who are newly arrived in the UK are least able to challenge a Home Office decision to detain them. The most recent figures available in October 2018 indicate that more than 27,000 people were detained in 2017. Some people are detained as soon as they arrive by Home Office officials at airports and ports, while others can be detained after living in Britain for many years when they try to renew work, family or study visas. A *Guardian* survey found 15 per cent were detained at a Home Office reporting centre, where immigrants must attend regular appointments while their applications are processed, and where they can find themselves starting the day queuing to see a bureaucrat and ending the day in a small cell with a stranger (McIntyre and Taylor, 2018). Others were apprehended during dawn raids at their homes, after rough sleeping, when found working illegally or while making applications for leave to remain (McIntyre and Taylor, 2018).

Lyons *et al.* (2017) point out that Britain is the only country out of the five European countries (the others being Germany, France, Spain and Italy) in the *Guardian* investigation that does not set a maximum time limit for holding asylum seekers in detention facilities and the only country that does not allow unaccompanied children who arrive and claim asylum the right to apply to be reunited with their parents. While the government announced it would end indefinite detention of immigrant families with children in 2010 and detaining unaccompanied children for more than a day was banned in 2014, unaccompanied children may still be detained during criminal cases and escorted during returns. In addition, families are still detained together in 'exceptional circumstances'. The *Guardian* survey uncovered 'multiple examples of children being detained in adult facilities' (McIntyre and Taylor, 2018).

In February 2019, annual government figures revealed that just 364 of 6,300 individuals who were identified by doctors and social workers as at particular risk of harm were subsequently allowed out of detention, representing just 6 per cent of detainees classified as 'vulnerable and at risk' after abuse including torture, sexual violence or trafficking (Townsend, 2019).

Victims of torture

Sile Reynolds (2018), Senior Policy Advisor at Freedom from Torture, points out that the 'hostile environment' 'has undoubtedly made it harder for asylum caseworkers to perform their functions to a standard that reflects the principle of refugee protection, the right to rehabilitation for torture survivors and respect for the rule of law'. 'It has driven policy and legislative measures', he goes on, 'that have redirected resources away from strained asylum casework teams and towards enforcement, indefinite detention and removal'.

Accordingly, the majority of Freedom from Torture's clients describe applying for asylum, in the UK as 'harrowing', since the determination of Home Office caseworkers to 'find the lie' in the applicant's account of past torture means that an individual's testimony is virtually worthless unless corroborated by a level of documentary evidence that is not available to all applicants and that, even when such evidence of torture is available, it is mishandled and dismissed by asylum caseworkers preoccupied with under-mining the credibility of the applicant (Reynolds, 2018). Sajid Javid, Reynolds (2018) concludes:

> could start with the most pronounced moral concern: Protecting torture survivors and asylum seekers from the 'hostile environment' and asking Home Office case workers to go in with a willingness to believe their stories.

That Javid will do this is unlikely, if his response to the fact that three or four dinghies had been found carrying cold, desperate migrants, including unaccompanied children, towards the UK coast (Godwin, 2018), is anything to go by.

Migrants crossing the English Channel

In an interview, after pledging that would-be migrants crossing the English Channel in small boats 'would see their asylum request processed "in the normal way"' (Press Association, 2019), Javid added that the journey across the world's busiest shipping lane was highly perilous and being undertaken by children as young as nine: 'It's incredibly dangerous, please do not do that, you are taking your life into your own hands' (cited in Press Association, 2019). He then issued this public pedagogy of threat to would-be migrants, immediately contradicting his 'normal processing' pledge by warning that it would be harder for such migrants to gain asylum:

Also, if you do somehow make it to the UK, we will do everything we can to make sure that you are often not successful because we need to break that link, and to break that link means we can save more lives.

(Cited in Elgot and Walker, 2019)

Colin Yeo, a leading immigration and asylum barrister pointed out that the Home Secretary's apparent threat was illegal: 'Sending genuine refugees to face persecution in order to dissuade others from seeking to come here is plainly illegal' (cited in Elgot and Walker, 2019). Yeo continued:

I imagine the home secretary knows this, but if so it is depressing that he is still saying it as a way of trying to make himself sound tough. The latest asylum statistics show that around three-quarters of Iranian asylum claims succeed, so we are talking here about genuine refugees.

(Cited in Elgot and Walker, 2019)

Labour backbencher Stella Creasy, who has visited migrant camps in Calais, accused Javid of normalising 'anti-refugee rhetoric online' and that 'People will continue to die and be at the mercy of traffickers all the time politicians pretend to play tough for votes rather than recognise why people flee' (cited in Press Association, 2019).

Lisa Doyle, director of advocacy at the Refugee Council, agreed about the illegality of Javid's threat: 'The 1951 refugee convention acknowledges that refugees may enter countries through irregular routes and should not be penalised for this' (cited in Elgot and Walker, 2019).

Doyle pointed out: 'The outcome of an asylum application cannot be pre-judged before it has been made and must be processed on its individual merit, irrespective of how that person reached the country.' 'Let us not forget', she went on, 'that we are talking about people who are in desperate need of protection, having fled countries with prolific human rights abuses' (cited in Press Association, 2019).

'It's a shame', she concluded, 'that the Home Secretary seems to need reminding that seeking asylum is a right and the UK has an obligation to assess claims fairly and grant protection to those who need it' (cited in Press Association, 2019).

Jon Date, Oxfam's head of government relations, also criticized Mr Javid's comments. He said:

Anyone who arrives in this country seeking safety from war or persecution should have their asylum claim considered. To reject it because we don't like the manner in which they arrive would be illegal and is an affront to fairness and decency. If the Home Secretary is serious about protecting lives, he should provide more safe options for people seeking asylum. This includes changing the restrictive rules on family reunion so that people with relatives in the UK can apply to live with them.

(Cited in Press Association, 2009)

Javid had abandoned a luxury safari holiday to 'get a grip' on what he described as 'a major incident' (Godwin, 2018). This largely successful attempt (it hit the headlines) to play 'the "race" card' came a couple of weeks before May's crucial Commons vote on her widely criticized Brexit deal. Writing in the *Independent*, Richard Godwin (2018) wonders:

perhaps the general cynicism of 2018 has infected my cheerful little heart, but I can't help wondering if the reason Javid cancelled his holiday was to create headlines about Javid cancelling his holiday, in order to open the 2019 news cycle with fresh new headlines about some sort of terrifying migrant flotilla that requires tough new measures from our safari-spurning home secretary?

As Godwin succinctly concludes, 'a little anti-migrant hysteria is hardly going to hinder Theresa May's anti-movement agenda, is it?' Godwin rightly argues that it is not that we shouldn't be concerned with human traffickers operating in the English Channel, but he doesn't 'remember any Tory ever cancelling a luxury sojourn to deal with, say, the universal credit catastrophe; or indeed Brexit', and, underlining the public pedagogical intent of the Conservative Party stunt, Godwin (2018) describes it as 'a production written, directed and orchestrated by the Tory party, starring you and everyone you know'.

Javid also queried whether the migrants were genuine asylum seekers:

if you are a genuine asylum seeker why have you not sought asylum in the first safe country you arrived in? Because France is not a country where anyone would argue it is not safe in any way whatsoever, and if you are genuine then why not seek asylum in your first safe country?

(Cited in Elgot and Walker, 2019)

In an interview on *Sky News* (2019a), around about the same time as Javid's query, Clare Moseley, CEO of CARE4CALAIS, which provides direct care for refugees in Calais, including food, clothing and camping equipment, offered an answer, when asked why they are trying to get to the UK. Their immediate problem, she explained is that they want to get out because conditions in Calais are very bad, with people sleeping rough with no shelter from the elements. They have come from the most danger-ous places in the world and are looking for somewhere safe to live and rebuild their lives. Asked why they are trying to get to the UK in par-ticular, Moseley pointed out that the majority of refugees who come to Europe do claim asylum in other countries: there are 1 million in Germany; half a million in Italy, and France processes 100,000 applications a year, a lot more applications than the UK:

> The specific thing about the refugees who come to Calais is they are the few who have a really strong reason for wanting to get to the UK, and the most common reason that we hear is family ties. Because the people who might have lost their families, lost everything in conflicts *do* have a remaining family member in the UK, they will do a lot to get to that family member.
>
> (Cited in *Sky News*, 2019a)

With respect to the dismantling of the so-called 'jungle' in Calais in 2016, Moseley explained that the French authorities are determined not to let the camps form, so if people have a tent, they get to sleep in it for two or three days before it is taken away from them: 'It's actually a lot worse than it was when the jungle camp was there, and God knows, that was bad enough' (cited in *Sky News*, 2019a). Estimating that there is about a thou-sand refugees across Calais and Dunkirk, so closing the camp did not work, nowadays Moseley states, people do not get to change their clothes, there is no sanitation and a lot of fungal disease (*Sky News*, 2019a).

Asked if by handing out care, food and tents, she is not encouraging people to come, and take the perilous journey, Moseley replied, 'I very much doubt that anyone would come to Calais and live in the mud and the squalor and the rain just for the second-hand clothes or the small bit of food that we give them' (cited in *Sky News*, 2019a). Moreover, she points out there is no academic evidence that pull factors exist. She stresses that we do know that there are massive push factors, and that it is these strong push factors that make people leave, such as persecution and terror, rather than economic reasons. Most of the people in Calais, she concludes, come from Syria, Afghanistan, Sudan, Eritrea and Iran (all ranked very low for peace and high for tensions, conflicts and crises,[2] so the Government needs to provide a safe and legal route to claim asylum. To press home the point, Moseley states that when the refugees were taken out of the Calais camp in 2016, in a fairly tough process, 86 per cent were granted asylum in France, and were therefore genuine refugees, and not 'economic migrants' (*Sky News*, 2019a).

Finally, in February 2019, it was revealed that, since Robert Mugabe was forced from power in November 2017, the Home Office has pushed ahead with a removals process for refused asylum seekers, many of whom have been in the UK for over a decade (Perraudin, 2019). Despite high-profile human rights abuses in the country, it has been working with the Zimbabwean Government to accelerate the deportation process to such an extent that, over the previous few months, Zimbabweans across the UK had been asked to attend interviews at Home Office centres. When they attended they found Zimbabwean government officials waiting to interview them. One woman, who has been in the UK for six years, said she attended one such interview and was told by a man speaking her native language, Shona, that she was 'one of thousands of Zimbabweans that the UK government wanted to remove from the country' (Perraudin, 2019). Having relatives who are politicians in the opposition Movement for Democratic Change, the official had a file on her with her photo and biographical details. Understandably, she commented: 'I am so anxious and I am so petrified. If the Home Office now is sharing my details with the Zimbabweans, then they are selling my life to them' (cited in Perraudin, 2019).

As if to back up the woman's claim, Andrew Nyamayaro, principal solicitor at Tann Law Solicitors, pointed out: 'Civilians are being tortured by members of the armed forces and the ruling party. Enforcing removals of Zimbabweans from the UK at this juncture is tantamount to sending someone to a death chamber', while Nyamayaro's colleague, Rumbi Bvunzawabaya, added: 'We have clients who are suicidal, who have been sectioned, since the news [about the interviews] came out. People are afraid' (both cited in Perraudin, 2019). Shadow Home Secretary, Diane Abbott responded: 'The government's resumption of deportations to Zimbabwe is in line with their hostile environment policy. The Home Office appear to have little regard for potential human rights abuses and are deporting people who may be at risk' (cited in Perraudin, 2019).

It would seem that, far from being over, the 'really hostile environment', routinely levelled at innocent people, is actually intensifying.

Health

A report by the Equality and Human Rights Commission (EHRC) conducted by Doctors of the World and Imperial College London, in collaboration with the Equality and Human Rights Commission and published on 29 November 2018, revealed that 'cost and fears about how they will be treated, or consequences for their immigration status, are preventing people seeking or refused asylum from using health services' (EHRC,

2018). This particularly affected pregnant women and disabled people (EHRC, 2018). Rebecca Hilsenrath, Chief Executive of the EHRC, commented:

> Everyone should have access to good quality healthcare, regardless of who they are and where they come from. People seeking and refused asylum are likely to have particular health needs because of past distressing experiences and the traumatic effects of fleeing to a different country. It's therefore crucial that they are able to fully and easily access healthcare and that their rights are protected by keeping healthcare separate from immigration enforcement. This is just about common humanity. We encourage the UK Government and healthcare providers to review this new research and take action on our recommendations to ensure health services are culturally appropriate, accessible to everyone and that staff are trained to recognise and respond to the specific needs of marginalised patients.
>
> (Cited in EHRC, 2018)

Consistent barriers to healthcare included: associated costs such as travel and prescriptions; the NHS charging policy in England, that does not apply in Scotland and Wales, being unaffordable; data sharing with the Home Office that meant asylum seekers were concerned that they may be arrested, detained or deported; no choice dispersal when accommodation is changed that disrupts healthcare and social networks; lack of knowledge of entitlements and eligibility (EHRC, 2018). In addition, some were worried that their health conditions, in particular those considered stigmatising such as HIV and mental health conditions, would be taken into account in the asylum process. Moreover, people who had traumatic pre-migratory experiences found it difficult to build trust in health professionals, with one stating that she avoids health services after being refused registration for an urgent appointment by a receptionist who said: 'Why do you worry? The Home Office gave you a house, and money for eating' (cited in EHRC, 2018). Finally, information provided to asylum seekers was not always accurate or in a language or format they understand, and often interpreters were not provided. This meant that many were unaware of their rights or how to assert them.

Dr Katherine Taylor, a GP and health advisor for Doctors of the World, concluded:

> People seeking asylum have fled war, conflict or persecution. Many will have experienced loss of or separation from family and loved ones, and some have gone for long periods without any healthcare.

When they arrive in the UK looking for protection, it's essential that they are able to get the healthcare they need.

(Cited in EHRC, 2018)

If granted refugee status

Once granted refugee status, asylum seeker support ceases, and refugees must apply for mainstream benefits and have 28 days to leave the accommodation provided to them by the Home Office. Because of the difficulties involved in applying for these benefits, very few refugees are able to register in this 28-day period, and are forced to go to food banks and charities for food and many also become homeless (Lyons *et al.*, 2017). As Judith Dennis, policy manager for the Refugee Council, put it:

> What we do is force [refugees] into homelessness and destitution almost routinely. It's hard to see how someone without an advocate or a special need that makes them a priority for council housing will be able to move on within 28 days. We would expect the majority of those who have to source private sector housing will become homeless.

(Cited in Lyons *et al.*, 2017)

The really hostile environment and women

Resonant with feminist arguments that public pedagogy in everyday life can be both oppressive and resistant (Luke, 1994, 1996; Sandlin *et al.*, 2011, 344), the following two examples show that the hostile environment impacts negatively on women, and the ways in which women are struggling against racism and patriarchy, sexism and misogyny.

Yarl's Wood Detention Centre

The official Yarl's Wood Immigration Removal Centre (this official description perhaps a more sinister public pedagogical sobriquet than the 'detention centre' of common parlance) website (Yarl's Wood, 2019) features a text box at the top of the page with the words, 'Respect, Support, Commitment. That's Our Promise' to the left, and a picture of six happy, smiling Asian women to the right. Below the text box, under the heading, 'Welcome to Yarl's Wood is the following description:

> Yarl's Wood IRC is a fully contained residential centre housing adult women and adult family groups awaiting immigration clearance. We

focus on decency and respect in all aspects of care for our residents and use continuous innovation to further improve and develop our service.

(Yarl's Wood, 2019)

Beneath that is an equally beaming white man, Centre Manager, Steve Hewer who states:

Our role is to provide a caring, yet safe and secure environment for all our residents at Yarl's Wood IRC. We do this by promoting Trust, Care, Innovation and Pride within the centre, and this is at the forefront of all our policies and procedures.

In his letter he assures readers that Yarl's Wood is unique in providing specialist and innovative services including:

- healthcare
- faith and cultural provision
- educational and recreational activities
- work opportunities aimed at supporting residents throughout their period of detention and preparing them for release and resettlement

(Yarl's Wood, 2019)

In August 2017, in a mixed report, Peter Clarke, HM Chief Inspector of Prisons, concluded after inspections in June of that year:

The leadership and staff could and should take much of the credit for the improvements, but it was clearly a frustration for them that the centre was not able to gain higher assessments in some areas of this inspection because of failings that were outside their control. For instance, weaknesses in immigration casework and health care provision, which had a significant negative impact on the experiences of detainees, were the responsibility of the Home Office and the commissioned health care provider respectively. If I had invested the energy and commitment to making improvements at Yarl's Wood that the current management team clearly have, I too would be frustrated.

(HM Inspectorate of Prisons, 2017)

May Bulman (2018) explains that the 400 plus held at the centre are there not because they have committed criminal offences, but because they need to establish their identities or facilitate immigration claims. As a visitor, not as a journalist, Bulman is there to meet Opelo Kgari, 27, who has been in Yarl's Wood for five weeks, and is one of the 120 detainees on hunger strike. 'It is quickly clear from the way she speaks and her ease of communication that she is very much British', Bulman explains. 'It's not a surprise. She came to the UK from Botswana with her mother when she was just 13 years old' (Bulman, 2018).

However, despite going through the British education system and achieving good A-level results, she was rejected when applying for an undergraduate degree at the University of the West of England due to her immigration status. Opelo had been thrown into Yarl's Wood twice in the year prior to Bulman's visit. The first time she had been on her way back from a short weekend in Belfast with friends when she was placed in a holding cell for two days – 'a memory that brings tears to her eyes – before being driven to the centre' (Bulman, 2018). The second time, after reporting to the Home Office as required every two weeks, she was picked up on her way to yoga and again locked in a holding cell for more than 12 hours with her mother, and then taken straight to Yarl's Wood at about 3 am, with only what she had on her back and no change of clothes (Bulman, 2018).

Bulman explains the background to the case. Opelo and her mother have been fighting for their right to stay since 2010. Having been refused asylum, they are arguing that, after living in the UK for 14 years, throughout Opelo's formative years, they have a human right to remain, yet 'despite ongoing legal proceedings, they find themselves locked in Yarl's Wood' (Bulman, 2018). However Opelo's main concern is fellow detainees, more vulnerable than herself who are not having their health needs met:

> There's one woman who spends all day walking around the centre with a packed handbag, claiming she had everything she needs in there. She's clearly not well. And there's an Iranian woman who's on suicide watch. Officers just sit outside her cell with the door open. She clearly shouldn't be in here at all. It's inhumane.
>
> (Cited in Bulman, 2018)

Opelo concludes, 'There are days when it's really hard and I feel like I have no future. I struggle to sleep'. 'The idea of going back to Botswana is unfathomable, she points out. 'I was never close to my family there and I don't even speak the language … I couldn't recognise myself as a non-Brit now' (cited in Bulman, 2018).

Towards the end of February 2018, nine months after Chief Inspector Clarke's castigation of the Home Office, Deputy Leader of the Green Party, Amelia Womack described her personal experience of a visit to Yarl's Wood:

I'll never forget my first visit to Yarl's Wood – one of our Government's brutal and inhumane detention centres. I had joined one of the many protests that gather in front of the building, making fleeting moments of contact with the incarcerated women. I saw handmade signs, waved through cracks in their open windows. I heard their voices call out to us, defiant in the face of their detention. And while we were separated by bricks and barbed wire, we were united in solidarity. Together, we would bring these walls down, and set these women free.

(Womack, 2018)

She continued:

As I write these words, over 100 women in Yarl's Wood are on hunger strike … today marks eight days of action against the injustices our Government is inflicting on them. They won't eat. They won't work. They won't participate in any way until the Government meets their demands.

Womack describes how, the day before, she had joined others outside the Home Office, demanding that the Theresa May Government listen to these women, and recognize their humanity. Womack went on, 'I have heard first-hand accounts of how some of these women are being treated, and the descriptions of their lives were heartbreaking':

Living under fear of their guards. Being separated from their families. Feeling powerless in a system, and never knowing when their hell would be over. Because, unlike every other country in Europe, we lock people up indefinitely, just because of their immigration status.

(Womack, 2018)

The woman I spoke to, Womack points out, called this purgatory. 'She didn't know how long she'd be there, if she'd be reunited with her partner in London.' She did not know 'if she'd be forcibly removed and deported from the country on one of the charter flights that sporadically take women from the centre with no warning. And this was just the tip of the iceberg.' The women's demands are clear:

- a 28-day limit to detention;
- adequate healthcare and mental health provision for detainees;
- a fair bail process;

- recognition by the Home Office that rape is torture (Womack, 2018). (Rape victims are detained despite a policy stating that victims of torture must not be detained for immigration reasons).
(Sharma, 2018)

Womack (2018) rightly notes: 'These are hardly radical demands and women shouldn't be forced to go on hunger strike to receive these basic rights.' However, the Home Office will not even meet with the women in Yarl's Wood. 'It is time', she concludes, for the Government to recognize 'that detention centres like Yarl's Wood are inhumane, costly and utterly unnecessary. Everyone deserves to be treated with humanity and dignity' (Womack, 2018).

Domestic violence

The 'really hostile environment' has had an alarmingly negative impact on migrant women (and presumably some men) experiencing domestic violence. The refusal rate for migrants applying to stay in the UK after suffering domestic violence more than doubled between 2012 (the year Theresa May initiated her 'public pedagogy of hostility') and 2016 (McIntyre and Topping, 2018). A new rule had been introduced in 2002 that gave people who entered the UK on a spouse visa, and then suffered domestic abuse, the right to apply for leave to remain (UN WOMEN, 2016). This was enacted, following representations from campaigners, who argued that women were being forced to choose between deportation and continued abuse or domestic violence (McIntyre and Topping, 2018).

However, as data journalist Niamh McIntyre and news reporter, Alexandra Topping, both at the *Guardian*, point out, a freedom of information (FoI) request by that newspaper revealed that the refusal rate for applications under the domestic violence rule rose from 12 per cent in 2012 to 30 per cent in 2016, the last year for which full-year data was available, with figures showing that 1,325 people were refused out of a total of 5,820 applications made between 2012 and 2016 (McIntyre and Topping, 2018). Rakhika Handa, legal policy and campaigns officer at Southall Black Sisters – a group of black and minority women with years of experience of struggling for women's human rights in the UK – comments on the effect of May's hostile environment since 2014, in dramatically exacerbating domestic violence:

We have this really hostile state climate where migrant women suffering domestic violence are being sacrificed at the altar of an immigration policy obsessed with limiting rights. That is not the hallmark of a civilised democratic society. We've been horrified by it.
(Cited in McIntyre and Topping, 2018)

Specifically, campaigners 'accuse the Home Office of using the testimony of violent husbands to deny victims of domestic violence the right to remain in the UK after they have escaped abusive relationships' (McIntyre and Topping, 2018).

In a key case in November 2017, the Home Office deported a woman who said she had been abused by her husband and his family, with a judge ruling that the Home Office had accepted his account 'without evaluation and then relied on it as the main reason for rejecting [the claimant]'s account' (Garden Court North Chambers, 2017, cited in McIntyre and Topping, 2018). Lucy Mair, a barrister from the law firm Garden Court Chambers who represented the claimant in the November case, pointed out that since 2015, people making applications under the domestic violence rule only have a right to an administrative review rather than an appeal. Thus, up until 2015, appeals had a very high rate of success. Since then, however, there is effectively no recourse to challenge a decision (McIntyre and Topping, 2018).

A FoI request, reported by McIntyre and Topping (2018), revealed that just 2 per cent of administrative reviews from 2015 to May 2018 resulted in an initial Home Office decision being overturned, just 15 out of 630 requests. By contrast, between January and March 2011, 82 per cent of appeals made under the old system successfully overturned a Home Office decision, according to evidence submitted to parliament by 'Rights of Women', a charity that 'specialises in supporting women who are experiencing or are at risk of experiencing, gender-based violence' (www.parliament, 2013, cited in McIntyre and Topping, 2018).

Thangam Debbonaire, Labour MP for Bristol West, who before becoming an MP worked for Women's Aid, and is a specialist in domestic violence, told McIntyre and Topping she was dealing with several cases where constituents were being forced to stay in abusive relationships because vital documents were kept by their partners. She went on, 'We have domestic violence laws which give out good signals – but what we are doing in these cases is saying we care about tackling domestic violence, except if you have insecure immigration status, and then we don't' (cited in McIntyre and Topping, 2018). Southall Black Sisters officer, Handa also points out that, 'Women who have been taken back to their home country and abandoned often have any documentation taken away from them' (cited in McIntyre and Topping, 2018).

As with all aspects of the 'really hostile environment', costs are prohibitively expensive (see Chapter 4, pp. 89–91; 94–95 of this book). If the victims cannot prove they are destitute, to apply to remain in the UK under the domestic violence rule has more than doubled since 2014 from £1,093 to £2,389 in 2018, plus an additional £2,389 for each dependent child

(Debbonaire, cited in McIntyre and Topping, 2018), thus reinforcing the anti-working-class motives of the Theresa May Government.

In February 2018, May issued a new policy document for Home Office staff that made it incumbent on officials to take into account the length of the couple's relationship and stated that police evidence against both parties should be considered. Handa summarizes its effects:

> We find that when the police are faced with cross-allegations from the perpetrator, if he says things like 'she attacked me/my mum/all of us and I was restraining her', police may arrest the woman or treat both perpetrator and victim the same,

and caution or warn them both (cited in McIntyre and Topping, 2018).

After a report by Claire Waxman, a victims' commissioner appointed by Sadiq Khan (Mayor of London, 2018), highlighting how people can be forced to remain in abusive relationships due to their immigration status, the Mayor and the Victims' Commissioner jointly called for:

- The reinstatement of legal aid for immigration cases to ensure those with insecure status can access independent advice and support
- Victims of violence to be entitled to financial support and safe accommodation in order to leave an abusive relationship, irrespective of their immigrations status
- Operational guidelines on how to respond to victims with insecure immigration status, including prioritising safety and support over immigration offences.

(Mayor of London, 2018)

Khan laid the blame squarely on Theresa May: 'The government's hostile environment policies are leading to vulnerable people being denied access to much-needed services and facing significant risk of being unlawfully detained' (cited in Mayor of London, 2018).

The Domestic Violence and Abuse Bill

On 21 January 2019, the first draft of the 'Domestic Violence and Abuse Bill' was published. Under it, types of *economic* abuse – such as restricting a partner's access to bank accounts or employment – will be recognized as a form of domestic abuse in England and Wales. Economic abuse also includes an abuser taking control of their victim's food, transportation – such as not allowing use of a car or housing – or deliberately damaging their credit ratings (*CNN*, 2019). Sian Hawkins, head of campaigns and public affairs at the charity Women's Aid commented:

> We know that economic abuse has not been very widely understood or treated as seriously, so it's really important that this new legal definition recognizes economic abuse as a key part of domestic abuse. It makes victims incredibly financially dependent on the perpetrators, and makes it difficult for them to leave an abusive relationship.
>
> (Cited in *CNN*, 2019)

In addition to economic abuse, the bill also: encompasses 'controlling and manipulative non-physical abuse'; prevents abusers from cross-examining their victims in court; introduces new protection orders; and establishes a national domestic abuse commissioner. Finally, it may force offenders to take mandatory lie-detector tests on release from prison (*CNN*, 2019).

With respect to migrant women, Amnesty International (2019) points out that, while under human rights law, the Government has a duty to protect every woman in the UK from violence, irrespective of immigration status, and while the Bill recognizes the need to overcome barriers to reporting for women with insecure immigration status, it offers little more than current provisions aimed at addressing the problem. The organization explains that guidance is already in place for police to support victims, but in reality police forces often share data with the Home Office and 'domestic violence victims are treated as suspects by immigration enforcement'. The Bill, it points out, introduces nothing on a statutory footing to prevent this from happening (Amnesty International, 2019). Moreover, according to Amnesty International (2019), instead of ensuring migrant women can access vital support services such as refuges, the Government suggests that some victims of domestic abuse 'may be best served by returning to their country of origin and, where it is available, to the support of their family and friends' (HM Government, 2019, 25, cited in Amnesty International, 2019).

The draft Bill includes the provision of £300,000 funding for BAME (black, Asian and minority ethnic) organizations that are supporting survivors of abuse. While Amnesty International (2019) welcomes the fact that the Government recognizes the need to support BAME organizations, such funding, it concludes, will go little way to support a sector that is hugely underfunded.

Step Up Migrant Women (SUMW) which comprises more than 30 organizations, including the Latin American Women's Rights Service (LAWRS), Southall Black Sisters, Amnesty International UK, Sisters For Change and the End Violence Against Women Coalition, also welcomes the Bill since the Government puts survivors at the heart of its plans. But it has urged the government to 'ensure equal protection for migrant, refugee and BAME women survivors of domestic abuse who often slip through the gaps because of their particular experiences of violence' (cited in Amnesty International, 2019). As Lucila Granada, Director of the Latin American Women's Rights Service, points out:

> The draft Bill offers little hope for migrant victims to access safety and support. This is particularly alarming, as the Bill itself recognises the 'significant vulnerability' of migrant victims who fear deportation as a result of coming forward. Every day we support women who are unable to trust that the police and the law will prioritise their lives and their safety simply because they are migrants. Deterring migrant women from reporting crimes gives impunity to perpetrators. We need a Bill that doesn't leave migrant women behind. We need safe reporting pathways, appropriate support, and a fair chance for migrant women to be able to break free from violence.
>
> (Cited in Amnesty International, 2019)

In the view of Kate Allen, Director of Amnesty UK, while in some ways the Bill is ambitious, many of the protections it provides will remain out of reach for some of society's most vulnerable women:

> Migrant women in abusive relationships are currently trapped and further victimised by their immigration status – excluded from financial support which often makes them reliant on their abuser and threatened with deportation should they seek support from the police. In its current form, the Bill barely tinkers at the edges of what is necessary to ensure migrant women are treated fairly. To truly be groundbreaking, the Bill must ensure all women can access housing and welfare support and report abuse without fear of immigration enforcement. Otherwise perpetrators will continue to use the immigration status of their victims as a weapon to control and abuse their victims.
>
> (Cited in Amnesty International, 2019)

Finally, Andrea Simon, Public Affairs Manager at the End Violence Against Women Coalition, commented on the need to abandon May's 'really hostile environment':

> The Government recognises that they must do more to protect domestic abuse victims with no recourse to public funds, but proposals announced today do not address or reverse the hostile environment

policies created by successive immigration bills, which create barriers to women seeking help and support and can be weaponised by abusers.

(Cited in Amnesty International, 2019)

Her conclusion underlines the cruel implications of Theresa May's obsession with cutting net migration:

> A truly victim-centred Bill would recognise that *all* women who've experienced domestic violence should have access to protection and justice regardless of their immigration status. This is currently not the case, because only some women can access the limited safety net offered by the government in the Destitution and Domestic Violence Concession. This shames us as a society – when we clearly put immigration enforcement over women's and children's lives.

(Cited in Amnesty International, 2019)

Underlining the efficacy of the arguments of feminist public pedagogy scholars that, while media representations reproduce dominant cultural forms, they can also 'circulate liberatory discourses and help produce among women and other marginalized populations collective identities oriented toward social justice activism' (Sandlin *et al.*, 2011, 344, following Dentith and Brady, 1998), the SUMW Coalition lists the following prerequisites for the Domestic Abuse Bill. It must:

- offer a system of full confidentiality, protection and support for all migrant women who report their abuse, regardless of their immigration status. This policy must apply to all statutory services, including the police and GPs;
- make specialist organisations led by and for migrant and black and minority ethnic women – which have had their services decimated by funding cuts – a central part of tackling domestic abuse and violence;
- recognise the gender inequality underlying domestic abuse and the disproportionate impact on women and girls;
- ensure refuge provision becomes a statutory obligation backed by national ring-fenced funding;
- ensure all migrant women at risk of experiencing abuse have access to public funds and routes to regularise their immigration status independent of their perpetrator.

(Cited in Amnesty International 2019)

With both protests at Yarl's Wood and the issues around domestic violence, we see how through a 'critical examination of daily experience and the complex interactions of government, media, and popular culture, public pedagogy creates sites of struggle' (Sandlin *et al.*, 2011, 344). In these sites of struggle, 'images, contradictory discourses, canonical themes and stories, and common sense versions of reality are disputed' (Dentith and Brady, 1999, 1), and grass-roots feminist public pedagogy fosters movement 'from positions of social inequality to ones of informed activism' (Dentith and Brady, 1999, 2).

Notes

1 Theresa May was Home Secretary up until 13 July 2016; thereafter Amber Rudd. Rudd carried on in much the same vein as May. Some, like Jeremy Corbyn, consider that, having inherited a 'failing policy', she actually made it 'worse' (cited in Grierson, 2018).
2 The Global Peace Index, which lists countries for levels of peace, had the following ranks for 2018. Syria was the least peaceful at 163 out of 163, and Afghanistan next at 162. Sudan was at 153; Eritrea at 138; and Iran at 131 (Institute for Economics & Peace, 2018).

4 The Windrush scandal, divided families and the Tory assault on family life

There was 'a conflation of people who were asylum seekers with people who were economic migrants, with people who were here with "leave to remain."' Theresa May 'wanted to exclude as many people as possible from the country, and, those who were here, she wanted to deport if she possibly could'.

(Norman Baker, Minister in the Home Office, 2013–2014,
BBC Newsnight, 28 February 2019)

Introduction

In this chapter, I begin by looking at an extraordinary event that came to light in 2018 and became known as the Windrush scandal. British subjects, mainly from the Caribbean, who had arrived in the UK before 1973, were detained, denied legal rights, threatened with deportation and some actually wrongly deported. I then consider families more generally who were or are divided, directly as a result of the effects of the hostile environment. I go on to examine what it actually costs in financial terms to obtain various UK visas, and ultimately for those who want it, UK citizenship. In the last section of the chapter, I outline my and my family's personal encounter with the hostile environment and our experiences of being in a divided family, and estimate the costs for us, both in financial and emotional terms.

The Windrush scandal

Commonwealth citizens who arrived in the UK after the Second World War and before 1973 are commonly known as the 'Windrush generation', after the ship MV *Empire Windrush* on which citizens from the Caribbean first arrived in 1948 (Home Affairs Select Committee, 2018, 5). The ship arrived at Tilbury, a town on the north bank of the River Thames, on 22 June, carrying 492 passengers from Jamaica, the first large group of

African-Caribbean migrants to arrive in the UK after the Second World War (Mead, 2007, 112). At the time, there were no immigration restrictions on people from Commonwealth countries entering the UK, their being known as the 'freely landed', who were allowed to live and work anywhere within the territories of the 'United Kingdom and Colonies' (Home Affairs Select Committee, 2018, 5).

Commonwealth migration continued throughout the 1950s and 1960s, with the Immigration Act 1971 confirming that those who were already present and settled in the UK when the Act came into force on 1 January 1973, and without any restriction on their leave, were entitled to stay indefinitely in the UK. The Act also recognized the right of wives[1] and children to join them, a right that was retained until the Immigration Act 1988 (Home Affairs Select Committee, 2018, 5).

Until the onset of the 'hostile environment', no Government had set out comprehensive policies to ensure that the 'Windrush generation' had their legal status fully documented. However, the subsequent introduction of policies requiring people to 'prove their right to be in the UK' in order to access essential services led to 'thousands of people being placed in a precarious position through no fault of their own' (Home Affairs Select Committee, 2018, 5).

As the Home Affairs Select Committee (2018, 5) points out:

> People have lost their homes and their jobs and been refused healthcare, pensions and access to social security. Not only did they not have documentation which proved their legal status in the UK but … it was made very difficult for them to gain it.

During its inquiry, the Committee heard how 'vulnerable people did not understand why they were told they did not have the necessary documentation – since they considered themselves British – or what they should do about it'. 'Many more', it goes on, 'tried unsuccessfully to prove their rights only to come up against the barrier of Home Office bureaucracy and poor decision making'. Moreover, some could simply not afford the fees (Home Affairs Select Committee, 2018, 5).

The Committee also expressed a concern that:

> a target-led approach may have led immigration enforcement officers to focus on people like the Windrush generation, who may have been easier to detain and remove than those less vulnerable, for example by detaining individuals such as Paulette Wilson and Anthony Bryan who clearly presented no risk of absconding.
>
> (Home Affairs Select Committee, 2018, 23)

Paulette Wilson

On 28 November 2017, Paulette Wilson, who had lived in the UK for more than half a century and had been paying national insurance contributions for 34 years, with a long history of working and paying taxes in the UK, spoke to the *Guardian*. Although she has indefinite leave to remain in the UK because she arrived before 1973, she received a letter from the Home Office in 2015, informing her that she was an 'illegal immigrant' and had six months before she would be sent to Jamaica, the country she left when she was ten and had never visited since. 'I was panicking. I was too scared to tell my daughter', she told the *Guardian* (cited in Gentleman, 2017a). Her housing benefit was stopped immediately, leaving her homeless, as were her sickness benefits. Her daughter Natalie started to support her financially and a friend let her stay in his flat. She was told to report monthly to the Home Office (Gentleman, 2017a).

Ms Wilson's mother had put her on a plane to the UK decades ago, to live with her grandfather, a factory worker, and her grandmother, a care worker. Her mother, who she never saw again, sent her here for a better life and, on the whole, Ms Wilson has been happy here. She never applied for a passport and never gave a thought about her immigration status (Gentleman, 2017a).

Ms Wilson spent a week at Yarl's Wood detention centre, before being sent to the immigration centre at Heathrow, where detainees are taken before removal from the UK. A last-minute intervention by her MP and a local charity prevented a forced removal. She was then allowed to return home (Gentleman, 2017a). Amelia Gentleman (2017a) gives us a glimpse of Ms Wilson's life in the UK:

> Paulette … arrived in the UK in 1968, went to primary and secondary school in Britain, raised her daughter … here and has helped to bring up her granddaughter. For a while, she worked in the House of Commons restaurant overlooking the Thames, serving meals to MPs and parliamentary security staff. More recently, she has volunteered at her local church, making weekly meals for homeless people.… The week of detention in Yarl's Wood was the worst experience of her life.
>
> 'I felt like I didn't exist. I wondered what was going to happen to me. All I did was cry, thinking of my daughter and granddaughter; thinking that I wasn't going to see them again' she told the *Guardian* reporter. Ms Wilson was taken from the Home Office reporting centre in Solihull, Birmingham, in a secure van and told she was going to be

sent out of the country: 'I couldn't eat or sleep; still now I can't eat and sleep properly'.

(Cited in Gentleman, 2017a)

When staff at Yarl's Wood told her she was being taken to the removal centre, she was allowed to call her daughter. She remembers screaming in terror down the phone: 'I was panicking because that evening they took away a lady. I watched her crying and being taken away. It was very scary' (cited in Gentleman, 2017a).

Natalie described the devastating effect the near destitution over a two-year period had on her mother: 'They have deprived her of everything … I am surprised we didn't lose her from the stress. She is normally so bubbly and sociable. Since she came out of Yarl's Wood she has withdrawn' (cited in Gentleman, 2017a). A few times in the last month, Natalie explained, her mother, who lives nearby, had come to her flat in the middle of night, waking her to tell her she was scared that Home Office workers were going to come to take her away, and that she couldn't sleep until she got into Natalie's bed (Gentleman, 2017a).

Ms Wilson's caseworker, who has dealt with as many as 40 similar cases of people who have lived here for decades but do not have British citizenship, spoke about the difficulties of dealing with the Home Office:

It's very hard to communicate with anyone in the Home Office. It's hard to get through on the phone and you never speak to the person making the decision because those numbers aren't provided. You're always talking to an intermediary.

In a response to Ms Wilson's MP, a member of the Home Office 'account management team' wrote: 'It may help to explain that Ms Wilson currently has no legal basis of stay within the UK and is liable to detention or removal' (cited in Gentleman, 2017a). She despaired at the pressure to prove that she was British, while the application to process leave to remain documents cost more than £240, money she did not have (legal aid being no longer available for cases such as hers). She was terrified that she could be separated from her family: 'I don't know anyone in Jamaica. I had no passport so I couldn't go' (cited in Gentleman, 2017a). Understandably, she does not like to be asked if she *feels* British:

I don't feel British. I am British. I've been raised here, all I know is Britain. What the hell can I call myself except British? I'm still angry that I have to prove it. I feel angry that I have to go through this.

(Cited in Gentleman, 2017a)

On 11 January 2018, the Government finally relented and gave Paulette Wilson official leave to remain in the UK (Khomami and Naujokaityte, 2018).

Anthony Bryan

Anthony Bryan's case is similar to that of Paulette Wilson. After 52 years continuously living in the UK, he was shocked to be told he was in the country illegally and faced forced removal. He had worked and paid taxes as a painter and decorator, helping to bring up his children and seven grandchildren (Gentleman, 2017b).

Towards the end of 2017, he was sent to an immigration detention centre and booked by Home Office staff on a flight back to Jamaica, a country he left when he was eight – the last time he flew on a plane – and has not visited since. It was only a last-minute intervention by an immigration lawyer that prevented his departure, and enabled him to be released from detention (Gentleman, 2017b).

Because he was so young when he came to the UK, he travelled on his older brother's passport, and had no documentation of his own. He had to stop work in 2015 when he applied for a British passport and the Home Office's immigration enforcement contractor, Capita, wrote to him informing him that he had no right to stay in the UK and would be removed (Gentleman, 2017b). This letter warned that 'his employer could face a £10,000 fine if they continued to employ him as an "illegal worker"' (Gentleman, 2017b). As Gentleman explains, Mr Bryan's situation is compounded by the fact that he has struggled with reading all his life, and has avoided form-filling: 'It's a stigma. It's hard to tell people that you need help' (cited in Gentleman, 2017b). Because of this, Mr Bryan has very few documents, has avoided registering with a GP, and has never opened a bank account, initially receiving his wage packet in cash (with tax deductions already made) and latterly having money paid into his partner's account (Gentleman, 2017b). Gentleman (2017b) outlines the stark reality of the 'really hostile environment':

> police and immigration officials arrived early on a Sunday morning with a battering ram, ready to knock down his front door (he opened it); he was held for two-and-a-half weeks in the Verne immigration detention centre, and told he would be sent back to Jamaica.

He was taken to Campsfield detention centre in November 2017, after an appeal was rejected. Bryan knows of others in the same situation:

I have at least three friends from secondary school in the same position, frightened to get a passport. They are worried that once they
apply for any documents, the same thing is going to happen to them. I
feel they could have treated me better than this after I've been here 52
years.

(Cited in Gentleman, 2017b)

Home Office setting up people to fail

In May 2018, Home Secretary Sajid Javid admitted in May 2018: 'there is
no question … that a number of people from that generation have been
mistreated', they 'have been seriously let down by the immigration
system' (Home Affairs Select Committee 2018, 5). After examining the
case files of Ms Wilson and Mr Bryan, the Home Affairs Select Committee accused the Home Office, saying it has 'set immigrants up to fail',
and that unless the system is overhauled the scandal 'will happen again,
for another group of people' (cited in Agerholm, 2018). The committee
pointed out that 'Thousands of people have been affected and denied their
rights – with 8,000 referrals to the taskforce, and over 2,000 documents
confirming status issued so far' (cited in Agerholm, 2018).

The previous month Dawn Butler, Shadow Equalities Secretary was
asked by *Sky News* whether Theresa May could personally be accused of
racism. She replied:

Yes. She is the leader that's presiding over legislation that's discrimi-
nating against a whole group of people who came from the Commonwealth, who suffered racism when they came over, the 'no blacks, no
Irish, no dogs'. And now they're having to relive that trauma all over
again because of Theresa May.

(Cited in Allegretti, 2018)

In the 1960s, such notices, or similarly racist variations on them, were
common when property was advertised for letting (Verma, 2018).

Shadow Home Secretary Diane Abbott, commented with respect to
recompense for those affected by the Windrush scandal:

It is an absolute disgrace that the government has still not come
forward with a clear plan for compensation, and is refusing a hardship
fund, even for people who have been made homeless or unemployed
by their policies. The government should act immediately on these
recommendations, including restoring immigration appeals and legal
aid, and removing the net migration target. But this scandal will

continue as long as the 'hostile environment' policy is in place, which treats people who are legally entitled to be here as if they are here illegally. This policy must go.

(Cited in Agerholm, 2018)

Windrush scandal continues despite Government apology

On 6 February 2019, a private Titan Airways jet left Birmingham carrying about 35 people, forcibly expelling them from the UK on a flight bound for Jamaica. It is the first such flight since the Windrush scandal came to light (de Noronha, 2019), leaving just hours before the 'Stansted 15' activists received suspended sentences or community orders, having been charged with terrorism-related offence for chaining themselves around an immigration removal flight in March 2017 (Gayle, 2019). As Luke de Noronha (2019), a writer and academic researching immigration control, racism and deportation, argues this is 'a reminder that lessons from the Windrush scandal have not been learned and that the government's hostile environment immigration policy endures'. According to Home Secretary, Javid, 'Every single person that will be on that flight that is being deported is a foreign national offender, they are all convicted of serious crimes, very serious crimes' (cited in de Noronha, 2019).

As de Noronha (2019) comments, 'It's not clear what the home secretary defines as "very serious" here, as it seems that some people on the flight have been convicted of minor offences'. He gives the example of Akeem, aged 22, who is registered blind and has epilepsy following a brain tumour as a child, and who served a four-month sentence for an assault conviction (de Noronha, 2019).

de Noronha (2019) correctly points out that whether they are (serious) criminals or not, deporting an individual after they have served their sentences amounts to a form of 'double punishment' and 'abandons all notions of rehabilitative justice'. It is also the case that many of the Jamaican nationals on the flight had lived in the UK since childhood, with some arriving as long ago as 1977. It also divides families since many on the flight have children who will likely be UK citizens. Moreover, some people booked on the flight have ongoing asylum claims and many simply do not know where they will go when they land in Kingston (de Noronha, 2019).

In the last chapter of this book, I consider the possibilities for a future society of free movement, beyond austerity, and a future world that is beyond capitalism itself. To conclude this chapter though, I turn my attention to a serious issue that tends to be overlooked by the media and is not a significant part of popular debate around the question of immigration: the dire predicaments of those families divided or torn apart because of the new vicious spousal legislation and rules that, as we saw in Chapters 1 and 2, are central to the 'really hostile environment'. As Imogen Lambert (2017) puts it, despite their cruelty, 'few will notice family immigration rules until it affects them, and when they do, people find it has the capacity to dictate their life – perhaps more than any other damaging government policy'.

Divided families

In a speech in the House of Commons about Brexit on 22 October 2018, Theresa May reiterated her 2016 election victory promise that what guides her every day are 'the interests … of ordinary working families'. As noted earlier in this book, but it cannot be stressed enough, this is true neither for the working class in general (e.g. Portes, 2018; Booth and Butler, 2018), nor for the individuals and families impacted by the hostile environment, as discussed in this chapter up to now. They have consisted of two categories of negatively racialized persons. On the one hand are those on the receiving end of non-colour-coded racism (xeno-racism as in the case of (Eastern) European migrants) and hybridist racism (primarily refugees and asylum seekers). On the other, there are those who have experienced long-term ongoing colour-coded racism, recently exacerbated by the Windrush scandal, namely those who emigrated from the Caribbean to the UK decades ago.

In Chapter 2, I analysed that part of Theresa May's public pedagogy of hate and threat, directed at families in which one partner was not a UK citizen, and the accompanying draconian changes in family migration rules, claimed to prevent, in her hostile rhetoric, 'sham marriages'. I now turn to a consideration of how the 'really hostile environment' affects these families. It should be pointed out that in such families, large numbers of whom are divided by spousal rules and regulations, it *may* be the case that the foreign citizen is not racialized in a negative way. However, for racists and others who are anti-immigration, the terms, 'immigrant', 'immigration', 'migrant', asylum seeker', 'refugee' and so on all signify in racialized discourse, masses of unwanted 'scroungers', 'trouble-makers' or 'people after our jobs', rather than human beings in need or in love. Families affected by the new spousal rules are, therefore, in their eyes, also part of 'the problem' that needs to be eliminated to get the numbers down.

May's determination to limit immigration by the 'family route' had an immediate and tragic effect. In March 2013, less than nine months since the rules came into effect, Donna Oettinger hurled herself in front of a train, clutching her three-year-old son, Zachery. The two were killed instantly. Imogen Lambert (2017), who has worked in the fields of social and economic rights in Cairo, explains the context:

> Donna was suffering with severe depression, but one of her burdens could have been relatively easily solved; the Egyptian father of her son, Mohammed Naser, was unable to join his family in the UK due to visa rules.

According to a friend, Donna and Mohamed met in Egypt five years before her death while she was on holiday and they moved in together.

> When she became pregnant, Donna returned to London, but Mohamed was not allowed entry into the UK. Her fragile state of mind: 'all came from the stress of her relationship. The bureaucracy got to her. They would not let him come over, even though he was Zaki's dad. They were not allowed to be together'.
>
> (Cited in Penrose and Wellman, 2013)

Fast forward four years, and on 17 December 2017, Paige Smith stood on a bridge above a road in north London: 'I don't remember too much, just standing there, looking over the edge, thinking 'I'm just going to jump', but then two police officers – I don't know where they came from – managed to talk me down' (cited in Doward, 2018).

As Jamie Doward (2018) explains, Ms Smith, aged 24, 'had been left suicidal by the Kafkaesque nightmare in which she and her Albanian fiancé, Fatjon Ballmi, 23, had found themselves since becoming engaged'. In September 2017, after having been together for nearly three years, they applied for a fiancé visa for Mr Ballmi. Two months later, the Home Office refused, claiming, incorrectly, that Ms Smith did not meet the £18,600 minimum income requirement (in actual fact it had lost a crucial payslip). Ms Smith was suffering mentally as a result of having been away from her fiancé for 11 weeks, and after attempting suicide was sectioned and kept in hospital for 24 hours (Doward, 2018).

An appeal judge took less than ten minutes to rule that the visa should be issued, with the Home Office taking another two months to confirm that it would not appeal. Ms Smith commented, once again confirming the actuality that the 'really hostile environment' extends way beyond so-called 'illegal' immigrants and is xeno-racist in intent and in practice:

> Everyone says 'you're a British citizen so you'll have no problem' when actually you do. But I'm yet to meet a British citizen who has an Albanian spouse who hasn't had a problem. I think certain nationalities

are extremely discriminated against when it comes to getting a visa. I guess it's part of the hostile environment. I know mistakes happen and it's a big government department but it seems to be happening far too often.

(Cited in Doward, 2018)

Further corroboration that social class as well as xeno-racism is central came from Ciaran Price of the Migrants Resource Centre:

Mothers, fathers, husbands and wives are being torn apart because the Home Office doesn't treat them as people with individual circumstances and needs. It doesn't seem to matter if your family has lived here for many years, or you have a seriously ill child, or, like 40 per cent of the population, you don't have a secure job that pays well enough to let you marry the person you fell in love with.

(Cited in Doward, 2018)

In another case that underlines the real intention of the hostile environment, in January 2018, Becky Darmon, 22, a British citizen, applied for a tourist visa for her Moroccan fiancé, Abderrahman Belafi, 26, an English language teacher, in order that he could be at the birth of their daughter. Ms Darmon explains: 'I had over £5,000 in the bank to support him and we'd booked the return flight' (cited in Doward, 2018). While she was aware that buying the ticket in advance was not advised, she pointed out: 'I know they say not to but if you don't they say there's no proof he's going home' (cited in Doward, 2018). In the event, their application was rejected at the time when Ms Darmon was 33 weeks pregnant: 'They said there was no proof he could afford the flight back home, even though we'd given them the ticket' (cited in Doward, 2018). As a result, Mr Belafi has only seen his daughter via his phone. To exacerbate an already callous and stressful scenario, she was born after an emergency C-section with very low iron levels and needing blood transfusions (Doward, 2018).

A few more instances will serve to exemplify how Theresa May seized upon the obviously very effective public pedagogy of the 'really hostile environment' in her relentless, obsessive and manic determination to reduce the net immigration figures to the tens of thousands. In the *Financial Times*, Robert Wright (2018) reported that when Tony Hiley married his long-standing partner Kyung in the UK in 2016, he expected few problems with obtaining his new husband's right to remain in the UK. Instead, the couple spent much of the previous 18 months in what they describe as a 'black hole', without receiving any information from the Home Office. In May 2018, not only was his application rejected, it was suggested that

Kyung should return to South Korea and that the couple could maintain their marriage via 'modern means of communication', such as Skype.

Campaigners have pointed out that the Home Office is refusing thousands of people the right to remain in the UK each year and telling families that, although they will be separated, the existence of phones, messaging apps, Facebook, and other Internet modes of communication makes the distance immaterial (Wright, 2018). Mr Hiley commented: 'It's ridiculous. If you suggest that to basically anyone, they'd laugh at you. Live your married life on Skype and Facebook? It's just laughable' (cited in Wright, 2018). According to the Joint Council for the Welfare of Immigrants (JCWI) the Home Office has used the Skype argument in nearly every case involving the splitting-up of families or other close relationships (cited in Wright, 2018).

Danielle Cohen, Mr Hiley and his husband's solicitor, stated that 'The Home Office assessment of what is proportionate is often poorly and unfairly applied', pointing out as particularly troubling the case of Filopater Zaki, a severely disabled 16-year-old from Egypt who lives in London with his mother and his uncle, who has lived in the UK for 27 years and is a British citizen. The uncle, Milad Shehata said that because his sister was separated from her husband, he was Filopater's only 'father figure', and that he assisted in basic tasks such as lifting Filopater into bed and into baths because he was so heavy (Wright, 2018). Notwithstanding, the Home Office wrote a letter stating that Filopater and his mother should return to Egypt and that they could maintain the relationship with family members by 'modern means of communication' (cited in Wright, 2018). Mr Shehata's response was that, because Filopater could move only his left hand, he would not be able to use most modern technology: 'I don't think if he goes back he will stay alive for long' (cited in Wright, 2018). In an anodyne response, typical of the Home Office, a spokesperson said that all cases were carefully considered on their individual merits, in line with the immigration rules and based on evidence provided by the applicant (Wright, 2018).

I will conclude this section of the chapter by recounting the experiences of Kisi Assan (not her real name). When she dropped off her two-year-old daughter at nursery in 2015, it was the first time they had been separated since the child was born (Townsend, 2018). Having received a summons from the Home Office, she then went off to attend a meeting at a nearby immigration reporting centre, having no idea that it was part of a plan to deport her at short notice to West Africa. On her way there, she had called her Home Office caseworker to say the trip was logistically difficult because she had to pick up her daughter. The official, she says, encouraged her to attend, promising to review the arrangement. On arrival, however,

Assan was told her deportation order had been certified, so there was no appeal. Court documents record that she began screaming and was restrained by eight security officials, with 'officers holding her legs, her arms and her head right back.' Handcuffed and with her phone taken away, Assan was taken to detention (Townsend, 2018). Mark Townsend (2018) describes the effects on the child:

> When her daughter's nursery closed, there was no one to collect her: the Home Office had arranged no care, and she was taken into emergency foster care. Court documents describe the child as in 'acute distress and confusion'.
>
> (Townsend, 2018)

It was nearly two days before Assan was told her daughter was in care, and another month before she saw her again. Case papers chronicle the meeting in Yarl's Wood: 'At first, [the girl] appeared uncertain and scared but then she recognised her. It was very confusing for [the child]' (cited in Townsend, 2018).

As Townsend (2018) explains, every year hundreds of children are separated when their mother or father is detained in a UK immigration centre – and numbers are going up. According to the charity Bail for Immigration Detainees (BiD), 322 children were separated from 167 parents between July 2017 and July 2018, up 16 per cent on the previous year (Townsend, 2018).

How many people are affected?

I have not been able to find any data on the actual number of families currently divided as a result of the 2012 legislation. However, towards the end of 2017, Amelia Hill (2017) pointed out that 'thousands of divided families are seeking support online over their stalled and blocked applications for spouse visas' and that social media groups are proliferating. The two most popular sites, I LOVE MY 'FOREIGN' SPOUSE, had 11,830 members, while UK SPOUSE VISA had 5,504 members (correct as at 28 November 2017). Other sites, including British Expats (Ongoing) had threads of more than 100 pages, where families share their anguish and beg for advice (Hill, 2017). What is clear is that numbers are growing. At the time of writing (13 February 2019), I LOVE MY 'FOREIGN' SPOUSE (Ongoing) has 15,279 members while UK SPOUSE VISA (Ongoing) has 5,646, a combined total of 20,925 people, and an increase of some 3,500 members in just over a year. British Expats (Ongoing) now has 3,571 pages of threads, a 3400 per cent upsurge. All this would appear to be a further indication that the hostile environment is not only alive and kicking, but flourishing.

There are also some figures from research commissioned by the Children's Commissioner, published on 9 September 2015, that relate to the number of children affected by Theresa May's obsession about lower immigration at any cost. At that time, it was estimated that up to 15,000 British children were growing up in 'Skype' families whose forced separation means that they use Skype as the only means of communication with the parent/step-parent/carer stranded overseas. As a result, many are reportedly suffering from significant stress and anxiety (Children's Commissioner, 2015).

The researchers found that the UK has the least family-friendly family reunification policies out of 38 developed countries, largely because families with only one parent/step-parent/carer who is a British citizen, as we have seen, need to earn a minimum of £18,600 per year to sponsor their partner's entry into the UK. This effectively means that around 40 per cent of British people who earn less are being warned not to fall in love with someone from abroad (Coombs, 2019). Co-author of the Children's Commissioner report, Helena Wray stated:

> Our research shows that the financial requirements are much more onerous than they need to be to protect the public purse and mean that British families cannot live together in the UK even when this is the only practical option. The result has been the separation of parents and children, heartache and misery. Some families cannot see how they can ever meet the rules and separation may be permanent. The rules urgently need to be made more flexible so that affected children, the vast majority of whom are British citizens, can grow up in their own country with both their parents.
>
> (Cited in Children's Commissioner, 2015)

The other co-author of the report, Saira Grant summarized its findings:

> We have found that the great majority of children adversely impacted by these rules are British citizens. They are being forced to grow up effectively in single parent families despite having two parents who want to be together because their British parent does not earn at least £18,600. The Government is under a legal obligation to treat the best interests of children as a primary consideration when implementing rules and policies. The current family migration rules fall woefully short of this and children's best interests are often reduced to a mere exception. In an ongoing attempt to reduce migration the Government has introduced rules which are now adversely impacting on British citizen families and children.
>
> (Cited in Children's Commissioner, 2015)

What does it all cost?

Visa, settlement and naturalization costs

Overall, though not as dramatic as in the past, the rates for settlement for 2018/2019 represent, in many cases, an increase on those for 2017/2018 of 4 per cent, more than double the inflation rate, as of January 2019 (Trading Economics, 2019). The price for settlement or indefinite leave to remain (ILR), which can only be applied for after five years in the UK, *even if the person is married to, or is a partner of a UK citizen*, is currently £2,389, and for a dependent relative it remains at a huge £3,250 (the application fee for a refugee dependent went down by £35 from £423 to £388). For naturalization or UK citizenship, it is now £1,330, and £1,012 for registering a child as British. So, to take the example of ILR, followed by UK citizenship, for a spouse and dependent child (as in my own personal situation), the current cost is a colossal £7,981. In addition, as well as the cost of visas, prior to settlement, some of which need to be made outside the UK, involving the expenses of travelling to country of origin, there are also fees for English language tests, NHS surcharges, the UK Citizenship Test, fingerprint fees and biometric residence card only available at limited venues, and so on.

As Colin Yeo (2018) points out, the Home Office 'makes a hefty profit on these fees' since the actual cost of processing an ILR application is £243 and a naturalization application costs the Home Office £372. 'Most outrageous', he goes on, 'is the application fee for registering a child as British', with the cost at £372.

From January 2019, the NHS surcharge at £400 is double that of the previous year. This supplement, introduced in 2015, applies to all those on limited (not settlement) visas, even if they are already working and paying taxes. As Bethan Staton (2019) points out, this includes 'NHS workers, families with children, and people who have been in the UK since childhood'. Those who have to pay it believe it could contribute to a new Windrush scandal, since those unable to pay could lose their status and become 'illegal' immigrants, risking being denied access to services or even deported (Staton, 2019). For example, Ijeoma Moore, a youth rights trainer, who arrived in Britain from Nigeria when she was two years old, has had to pay the surcharge every year, since it was introduced as part of a ten-year route to citizenship. In addition to the surcharge, whose increase she describes as 'terrifying', she has to pay Home Office visa fees of £1,033 every two and a half years. As she puts it, 'You're constantly saving. It feels really unfair. It makes you feel like an outcast' (cited in Staton, 2019).

Donna Kinnair, general secretary of the Royal College of Nursing, told *Sky News* that the fees were 'immoral' and could 'tear families apart':

> While overstretched health services cope with 42,000 nursing vacancies, the government is creating more barriers for international nurses by doubling the charge they must pay to work in the UK. They already contribute financially through National Insurance and taxation, not to mention the work they do to care for us and our loved ones. The extra charges required by the surcharge are the last thing they need.
>
> (Cited in Staton, 2019)

The response of the Home Office served to underline the enduring and ongoing nature of the 'really hostile environment', and was accompanied by public pedagogy that could operate as a justification for privatising the NHS by stealth, since the surcharge increases much-needed money for 'sustaining and protecting' the UK's healthcare system:

> We welcome long-term migrants using the NHS, but we believe it is right that they make a fair and proportionate contribution to its long-term sustainability. Parliament agrees and has approved the order we proposed to increase the immigration health surcharge so it better reflects the actual costs to the NHS.
>
> (Cited in Staton, 2019)

New immigration rules and legal costs

Data analysts writing for the *Guardian* (Bozic *et al.*, 2018) have calculated that Home Office officials made more than 5,700 changes to the immigration rules between 2010 and August 2018, meaning that the rules have more than doubled in length to almost 375,000 words, making the visa application process nearly impossible to navigate, according to senior judges and lawyers. In 2012 alone, coinciding with the introduction of the 'really hostile environment', more than 1,300 changes were made (Bozic *et al.*, 2018).

Colin Yeo (cited in Bozic *et al.*, 2018) has noted that 'the rules are so precise' that it has become essential to use a lawyer, forcing applicants to pay 'astronomical' legal fees. Moreover, attempts to eliminate discretion from the rules since 2012 have instead 'removed any human element, humane judgments', making it a 'computer says no' exercise, and making it even difficult for judges and lawyers. The changes are also hurriedly drafted, making them badly written with a number of errors (cited in Bozic *et al.*, 2018). With the preceding analysis in this book in mind, one can imagine Theresa May's obsession with getting numbers down to 'tens of thousands' behind the rush.

It is also easy to imagine that the complexity of the rules might be to deter applications being made, with the cost of solicitors added to the already excessively high government charges making the endeavour downright financially impossible for many, or further disincentivizing (potential) applicants. Another related effect of the changes is the loss of appeal rights introduced in the Immigration Act 2014 (see pp. 31–33 of this book). According to Yeo, this has resulted in 'far less scrutiny of the Home Office': 'Decision makers know nobody's looking over their shoulder and no judge is going to review their decision. In many cases, the refusal rate has risen.' Yeo called for a 'substantial rewrite' of the rules (cited in Bozic *et al.*, 2018).

The 'really hostile environment': a personal testimony

> You can have your passport back to visit him in hospital, but you'll have to start your visa application all over again.
> (Communication from the British Embassy, Phnom Penh, early 2012)

I need to stress here that I believe firmly that, since the demise of the era of primitive communism (Engels, 1884; Marx, 1894 [1966], 831), history has been driven by a dialectical struggle between the imperatives of the respective ruling classes and those of corresponding exploited groups, rather than the whims and personal obsessions of individuals, however amoral and self-serving are their destructive intentions. However, it would be dishonest to deny that writing this book has been cathartic in exposing the degree to which Theresa May's callous and cruel 'really hostile environment', which, as I argued in Chapter 1, has a definitive economic and political backdrop, and has impacted negatively on so many people, including myself and my nuclear and extended families.

Setting the scene

After just six months of marriage, in June 2010 the person who was then my wife left me without prior notice, having seized the opportunity while I was on my way to work. A few months earlier, over 6,000 miles away, Lyka's partner, also Meoun's biological father, had walked out on them (Meoun is not her real name).

Fast forward a year, just as I was getting over a very acrimonious and traumatic divorce, I got a phone call from my elder daughter, telling me that my only son Dave had died in tragic circumstances in Bangkok. On the day of his funeral, one of his closest friends, Tom, and I vowed to take the trip that Dave had been unable to complete (Dave had been waiting for Tom in Bangkok to travel to Laos and Cambodia).

It was in Phnom Penh, travelling with Tom in August 2011, that I met Lyka and entered into a romantic relationship with her. Lyka had worked very long hours on pittance wages in garment factories for most of her working life to provide care for Meoun (for Lyka's account of factory life, see Thorn, 2013). Shortly after meeting Lyka, I went back to the UK with Tom, but returned to Phnom Penh in September 2011 to see her. We have lived together continuously since then. It was not until May 2018, however, that Lyka and Meoun obtained UK citizenship, even though Lyka and I got married in the UK in 2012, and I have supported Meoun financially and in every other way, since. I first met Meoun, then aged three, on my second trip to Cambodia. The length of time it took to get citizenship, and the inconveniences, financial and personal hardships in the account that follows are direct results of Theresa May's 'really hostile environment'.

Our struggle[2]

In October 2011, we applied in Phnom Penh for a visitor's visa for Lyka to come to the UK at my expense (maximum stay six months) and were turned down on the grounds that, in the words of the entry clearance officer: 'I am not satisfied on a balance of probabilities that ... you intend to leave the United Kingdom on completion of your visit'. Having more than enough money to finance the visit, and having provided full details of my financial and professional status, I was surprised that I was being accused of lying to the British Embassy in Phnom Penh, and potentially also being accused of being complicit in an attempt to break UK immigration law. Not only had such a thing never crossed my mind, I felt personally slighted because, given that I was sponsoring Lyka because I knew her well enough to trust her, my integrity was being undermined as well as hers. Nothing like this had ever happened to me before, but it was just the beginning of a long process of our having to prove that we were not lying, rather than the Home Office having to prove that we were. We applied again for a visitor's visa in January 2012.

Shortly afterwards, I was air-ambulanced, courtesy of my travel insurance policy, with (symptoms of) heart failure from Phnom Penh to Bangkok, where, I was told, the facilities I needed were available. I can only surmise that my poor health was, in part, the result of my divorce and the unexpected death of my son. Lyka asked the British Embassy in Phnom Penh if she could have her passport back to visit me in hospital, and was told that she could but she would have to start her visa application all over again. Could it be that the Embassy was already on alert for the imminent implementation of the hostile environment? I was in bed for a week, while they brought my heart rate down. Not recovering as fast as the cardiologist had hoped, on release from hospital my only hope was that I would be with Lyka at least until the following Christmas.

The second visitor's visa application was successful and Lyka came to the UK with me in February 2012 for about five months, after which time she was required to go back to Phnom Penh to apply for a spouse visa, because it cannot be applied for in the UK. We had already decided to get married a long time before our wedding on 8 July 2012. However, not being aware of the *details* of Theresa May's forthcoming changes in family immigration rules that came into effect the day after our marriage (9 July 2012), we decided to get married urgently.

Lyka had, of course, not seen her daughter for the duration of her first visit to the UK together, and we had become a 'Skype Family' (see pp. 86, 88 of this book). After getting married, we returned to Phnom Penh, spending about three months there, waiting for the spouse visa, before obtaining it in October 2012. This was just as well, since we had not envisaged waiting so long for the visa, and were literally running out of money to the extent that, out of desperation, I was contemplating flying to Bangkok and back to withdraw money there on the only card on which I still had credit (that card was not accepted in Cambodia). We returned to the UK, once again in October 2012 without Meoun, with vivid memories of the heartbreak of being in a divided family, as Meoun was crying all the way to the airport.

We returned to Phnom Penh in March 2013 to apply for an initial visa for Meoun to come to the UK. We obtained this in early May, and we all returned to the UK where we stayed for about a month before taking Meoun back to Phnom Penh, on the advice of our solicitor, in June 2013, so that she could return to school in Phnom Penh, having taken a month off to come to the UK. We stayed for about a week, and once again had the trauma of leaving Meoun at the airport in Phnom Penh with our extended family. Although, six months older than the last time we had to leave her at the airport, at age five, Meoun was not fully cognisant of course as to what was happening to her life, and we said our goodbyes with her sobbing and clinging on to her mother, before boarding the plane.

We resorted to being a Skype family again from June 2013 until late October when we returned to Phnom Penh once again to apply for a 'to join mother' visa which we obtained in December 2013. From then on, Theresa May's new family visa rules allowed us to apply for subsequent visas in the UK, but we had to wait until July 2015, two and a half years before applying for and obtaining 'leave to remain' for both Lyka and Meoun in July 2015. There followed another two-and-a-half-year wait to obtain 'indefinite leave to remain', and after that UK citizenship and UK passports. All along the way, we had to *prove* with documentation (including photographs of us together) that we were not, to use Theresa May's terminology, in a 'sham marriage' or a sham family. At least we did not suffer the humiliation of having our wedding ceremony interrupted so we could be questioned about our 'sex lives', or a dawn raid to check if we were sharing a bed, or told that our relationship was not genuine because we were wearing pyjamas in bed. Nor did we have our number of toothbrushes checked (Taylor and Perraudin, 2019)! Finally, our marriage was not delayed for up to 70 days, nor was my wife 'detained for months' on suspicion of being in a 'sham marriage' (Taylor and Perraudin, 2019). Information obtained by the *Guardian* through a freedom of information request shows registrars sent 2,868 section 24 reports – which alert the authorities to a potential sham marriage – in 2018, a 40 per cent rise from 2,038 in 2014. Lawyers said registrars had become 'infected with the culture of the hostile environment' (cited in Taylor and Perraudin, 2019). For further indications that the 'really hostile environment' is currently being cranked up, see pp. 98–99; 101–103 of this book. Prior to 2012, officials just needed to be satisfied that the marriage was genuine.

The six and a half years of anxiety about whether Lyka and Meoun would eventually get UK citizenship were tempered by the certainty that, were they to be refused, I would go to live with them in Cambodia, not an option open to the vast majority of divided families.

Our costs

Here is an approximate breakdown of what it all cost financially:

> Total visa costs, Lyka and Meoun: £9,000
> Total solicitor' fees: £2,800
> Flights: £9,000 (11 returns)
> Hotels in Phnom Penh: £11,000 (10 months)
> Subsistence in Phnom Penh: £15,000 (10 months)
> Total: nearly £47,000

We were able to pay this exorbitant amount, solely because my financial status was such that I was able to get into considerable debt, and just about survive it.

The adult dependent relative rules

Since Theresa May's July 2012 immigration rules, it has been virtually impossible, in practice for adult dependent relatives to get leave to remain in the UK (see p. 27 of this book; and for full details, see Yeo, 2017). In the event that a dependent relative does, or relatives do, get leave to remain on human rights grounds (initial cost, £2,622), the granting of indefinite leave to remain takes a phenomenal ten years, and UK citizenship a further year after that. The ensuing costs for a couple are nearly £20,000 at 2019 levels to obtain UK citizenship after being granted leave to remain, amounting 'to ten years of indentured servitude to the Home Office' (Vassiliou (2019) provides an example and breakdown of costs).

The rules give no weight 'to any emotional ties that might exist between older people and their adult children and grandchildren' (Vassiliou, 2019). Thus, though in our case the ties with our Cambodian extended family are very strong – Lyka's mother and father had looked after Meoun for the many years that she worked in the factories, and I have a very close relationship with the whole extended family, for whom I have been the main financial supporter since 2012 – having her mother and father come and live with us (even though we wanted to) was ruled out. Instead, we applied for a visitor's visa for Lyka's mother. This was met in March 2016, with the familiar response:

> I am not satisfied on the balance of probabilities that you are genuinely seeking entry as a visitor for a limited period or that you intend to leave the United Kingdom at the end of the visit ... there is no right of appeal or right of administrative review.

After four years of successfully 'proving' to the authorities that our intentions were honest, we were once again being accused of lying and colluding in so-called 'illegal immigration'. Such is the nature of the 'really hostile environment'. Notwithstanding occasional visits to Cambodia, until the demise of the Theresa May Government we have resigned ourselves to not even contemplating anything beyond remaining an extended family via Skype for the foreseeable future.

Notes

1 Husbands were not allowed entry until changes made in 1974 (see *Hansard* (1974) for the second reading of the Spouses of United Kingdom Citizens (Equal Treatment) Bill.
2 While reading this section, the reader may like to refer back to the heading, 'Spouses and partners' in Chapter 1 of this book – see p. 26.

5 The escalation of racism, the crisis in neoliberalism, and public pedagogy for a borderless socialist future

> The movement of peoples across the globe will mean that borders are almost going to become irrelevant by the end of this century as existing borders are being ignored, and a borderless world is inevitable.
>
> (John McDonnell, cited in *BBC News*, 2016)

Introduction

In this final chapter, I begin by posing the question, are the effects of the hostile environment intentional? I then consider whether the hostile environment is crumbling or being ramped up. Next I look at the escalation of racism more generally in the context of the hostile environment. I move on to a discussion of what many see as a crisis in neoliberalism, a crisis that is receptive and potentially conducive to the promotion of public pedagogies for socialism. Accordingly, I then make the case for what I consider to be the urgent need for a left-led Labour Government. In so doing, I outline what such a government might look like before concluding by briefly making the case for a socialist future without borders.

Are the effects of the hostile environment intentional?

Given Theresa May's blinkered obsession with reducing net migration at any cost, it is quite likely that the effects of the hostile environment – the consequences of her public pedagogies of hate and threat, the impact of the callousness of her vitriol on individuals and families, divided or not – did not merit consideration. In Chapter 2 of this book, I cited Jamie Grierson (2018) who was of the view that only Theresa May knew in 2012 that her hostile environment would evolve into a catch-all approach to migrants, 'illegal' or otherwise. The Joint Council for the Welfare of Immigrants (JCWI) and social justice group, Liberty are less circumspect.

On 23 April 2018, they jointly called for the appointment of an Independent Commission to review the workings of the Home Office and the legal framework of the 'hostile environment', at the same time publishing a *Dossier of Failure*, detailing the need for an Independent Commission into the systematic failures that culminated in the Windrush scandal. The dossier followed a private meeting with May, in which she made it clear that she had no intention of properly dealing with the scandal, instead using the meeting to try to get the JCWI to back the Home Office (JCWI, 2018). Satbir Singh, Chief Executive of JCWI, commented:

> It is not my job to rehabilitate the shattered reputation of the Home Office. It is an indictment of just how out of touch Theresa May is with the outrage her actions have caused that No. 10 could expect JCWI to put out a statement in support of their actions, while they still cling to her hostile environment. The treatment of the Windrush generation is no accident. It is precisely what happens when an anti-immigrant dogma takes over at the Home Office. Despite warnings, Theresa May chose to create a system that was designed to be as hostile as possible, whatever the cost. What on earth did she think the consequences would be? Families have been torn apart, left destitute and removed or thrown into detention without due process. It is no surprise that assurances from the Home Secretary now have such limited credibility. Only a full, independent inquiry into Home Office policy and practice will help restore that trust.
>
> (Cited in JCWI, 2018)

The *Dossier of Failure* establishes:

- The Home Office's deliberate intent in creating the hostile environment which resulted in the Windrush scandal;
- That the Home Office knew before and after they implemented the hostile environment that it would result in problems for people legally resident and British citizens who didn't have the right documents;
- The Home Office's failure to heed multiple warnings about the harmful impact of the hostile environment;
- The Home Office's failure, despite recommendations, to monitor the impact of the hostile environment;
- That Home Office decision-making is error-prone and often arbitrary;
- That the government has repeatedly tried to reduce scrutiny and corrective mechanisms in the Home Office, rather than dealing with problems.

(JCWI, 2018)

On 19 April 2018, Green MP, Caroline Lucas tabled an Early Day Motion (2018), calling on the Government to establish an independent commission to review Home Office policies and practice on immigration (JCWI, 2018).

Further evidence of Theresa May's *personal* intention to roll out the 'really hostile environment' to as many people as possible, irrespective of so-called 'illegality', has been provided by Norman Baker, Liberal Democrat Minister in the Home Office in the ConDem Government between October 2013 and November 2014, when of course May was Home Secretary. Asked about the attitude towards immigration at the time, he referred to 'endless conversations on a weekly basis as Theresa May wanted to tighten every single screw she could find on the immigration system'. He went on to refer to 'a conflation of people who were asylum seekers with people who were economic migrants, with people who were here with "leave to remain"', and that her problem with immigration was that 'she wanted to exclude as many people as possible from the country, and, those who were here, she wanted to deport if she possibly could, including those who were of economic value to us' (*BBC Newsnight* on YouTube, 2019).

Is the hostile environment crumbling or being ramped up?

Theresa May's 'really hostile environment' is under attack from a number of quarters. We have already seen how Sajid Javid has tried to diffuse opposition to it by renaming it the 'compliant environment', a term mouthed by May herself in her interview with Andrew Marr (see pp. 47–48 of this book). We have also seen how people have struggled against it. As a result, some of its particularly severe features have been withdrawn, or are likely to go: the 'deport first, appeal later' policy (see pp. 31, 40) (*BBC News*, 2017); the Department for Education (DfE) pupil data-sharing deal with the Home Office (Weale, 2018b); the checking by banks on the status of new applicants and existing customers (Usborne, 2018); the Home Office scheme that used NHS data to track migrants (Bowcott, 2018); and the 'Right to Rent scheme' requiring landlords to check the immigration status of immigrants has been declared a breach of human rights laws by the High Court (see GOV.UK (Ongoing) for updates on immigration legislation). Yet, as Usborne (2018) argues, 'such actions barely touch the web of interwoven legislation, administrative policy and a default position of suspicion that is invisible to most of the public, but has been tightening for years'. 'The reality', as Gracie Bradley of Liberty, points out, is that unless people work in the affected professions or are subject to these measures, very few have any idea how deeply embedded they are. I think that's why the government thinks it can potentially get away with calling it 'compliant' now.

(Cited in Usborne, 2018)

Nearly a year after Theresa May apologized for the treatment of those affected by the Windrush scandal, in early 2019 a damning parliamentary report revealed that Home Office officials continued to display a lack of urgency in their response to the crisis. No information was available as to when a compensation scheme would be launched, while many of those affected were in dire financial circumstances caused by periods of enforced unemployment, removal of unemployment benefits, and debts run up trying to pay legal bills and Home Office fees. Some remained homeless. There was also a concern that people from non-Caribbean countries, such as Nigeria, were struggling to get help from the Windrush scheme because people had assumed they could not be part of the Windrush generation because they did not arrive on the *Empire Windrush* itself (Gentleman, 2019).

The hostile environment and the general escalation of racism

de Noronha (2019) makes a connection between one kind of 'hostile environment', 'aggressive immigration policies' and another, 'stop and search' that continues to target black people disproportionately (Dodd, 2019):

Racism at the border is inseparable from racism within Britain; they license and feed off one another. For black and brown British citizens, that familiar refrain, 'Go back to your country', captures this most clearly.

(de Noronha, 2019)

Not only has the hostile environment's primary function remained fully intact, not only has it undeniably spread to *all* immigrants and to UK citizens, the hostile environment has also intensified racism in general terms, upping the barometer of colour-coded racism, of xeno-racism and hybridist racism. As Dawn Butler (2018) argues, while the Theresa May Government has reported on its 'race disparity audit', in truth, this just tells us what we already know – that people from diverse communities face multiple layers of disadvantage. A few examples will suffice. In 2016, as Butler (2018) points out, in May's first year as Prime Minister not a single person of black Caribbean origin won a place on a prestigious graduate scheme for Whitehall civil servants – despite a record number of applicants – 339, nearly double that of the previous year. This was also the first time in five years that that there was no representation from that minority ethnic group in the cohort (Waugh, 2018).

Moreover, NHS data shows that people in the 'black ethnic group' were the most likely to have been detained under the Mental Health Act in 2016–2017, and people in the 'white ethnic group' the least likely. In addition, black Caribbean people had the highest rate of detention under the Mental Health Act 1983 (GOV.UK, 2018).

In 2019, research revealed that black Britons and those of South Asian origin face 'shocking' discrimination in the labour market at levels unchanged since the late 1960s. The study by researchers at Oxford University found that applicants from minority ethnic backgrounds had to send 80 per cent more applications to get a positive response from an employer than a white person of British origin. The researchers sent almost 3,200 applications to both manual and non-manual jobs, advertised on a popular recruitment platform between November 2016 and December 2017 (Siddique, 2019). In a presumed reference to Theresa May's 2016 prime ministerial victory statement – her pledge to combat 'burning injustice' – co-author of the research, Anthony Heath commented:

> The absence of any real decline in discrimination against black British and people of Pakistani background is a disturbing finding, which calls into question the effectiveness of previous policies. Ethnic inequality remains a burning injustice and there needs to be a radical rethink about how to tackle it.
>
> (Cited in Siddique, 2019)

de Noronha (2019) makes pertinent links between racism, gender, disability and social class in the light of ongoing arguments about individuals' worth based on their contributions to society in times of austerity:

> As long as the defence of immigrants relies on proving their contribution, people who deserve support will be excluded. Instead, we need to challenge the broader system of austerity and racist criminal justice that restricts the possibilities for 'contribution' in the first place. After all, 'contribution' doesn't work for marginalised British citizens either – for welfare claimants, for those unable to work because of disability and ill health, and for those performing essential and yet unpaid social reproductive and caring roles (mostly women, of course).
>
> (de Noronha, 2019)

With further public pedagogy pertaining to the nature of capitalist 'divide and rule' tactics, he concludes by underlining the ruling-class need to highlight scapegoats to detract from the ongoing austerity measures:

> Moral panics about migration, crime and security work to obscure widening inequalities and deepening insecurities. As ever, it appears that by nurturing nationalist resentments about racialised outsiders – the 'criminal', the 'migrant' … the government is able to redirect public anger, and secure consent for the very policies that make life more difficult and uncertain for the vast majority.

'As the UK recommences these brutal and secretive mass deportation flights', he goes on, 'we need to expand our critique of the hostile environment'. We also 'need to be brave enough to 'condemn reducing human beings to criminals, and to depart from the logic of judging people based on their contribution', since the 'criminal justice system is racist; racism at the border articulates racism within; and in the context of relentless austerity, "contribution" is a dead end'. These are the arguments we need to make 'if we really want to see an end to the hostile environment' (de Noronha, 2019).

I will conclude my observations on the 'really hostile environment' by demonstrating its contemporary, essentially Orwellian and enduring nature. Since 2016, the Home Office has been attempting to embed immigration officers at an hourly rate of £58.20 (a cost that it claims it can make back by charging for or denying services) as part of an 'enhanced checking service' offered to public bodies, including NHS trusts and local authorities, and private firms (Savage and Cadwalladr, 2019). This is in addition to its 'core offer of free (mainly online) guidance and checking services to private and public sector organisations' (Home Office, cited in Savage and Cadwalladr, 2019), as Michael Savage and Carole Cadwalladr (2019) explain:

> The organisations are offered 'real-time' access to information about someone's immigration status through an 'on-site immigration official', who can be asked to attend interviews and encourage undocumented migrants to leave the country voluntarily. The embedded official can also pass the details of undocumented migrants to immigration enforcement officers.

Effectively risking discouraging migrants getting services they need, sometimes desperately, its intention is to make sure that migrants are either charged for services or denied access to them, if they fail to prove they are in the country 'legally' (Savage and Cadwalladr, 2019). In the words of one of the documents seen by the *Observer* newspaper:

> Ensuring that immigration status checks are conducted prior to an individual obtaining benefit or services is an essential part of ensuring illegal migrants cannot access public services to which they are not entitled, encounter a compliant environment which encourages [voluntary] departure and limit the harm they cause to the taxpayer.
>
> (Cited in Savage and Cadwalladr, 2019)

As David Lammy, the Labour MP who led the criticism of the Windrush scandal, correctly notes, 'Sajid Javid announced he had paused the hostile environment in July, but this shows it is being ramped up'. 'The Home Office', he went on, 'should come clean about the details of this secretive scheme, and explain how it justifies spending £58.20 an hour to fill our hospitals and councils with border guards' (cited in Savage and Cadwalladr, 2019).

Diane Abbott added:

> This Tory government is not fooling anyone by rebranding their hostile environment policies as a 'compliant environment'. By gathering information in this way the Home Office is creating distrust in our public services, and risks deterring vulnerable families from accessing vital support.
>
> (Cited in Savage and Cadwalladr, 2019)

Finally, Satbir Singh, the chief executive of the Joint Council for the Welfare of Immigrants, stated:

> Spreading the tentacles of this hostility ever deeper into our hospitals and public services is a chilling new development. It will push people away from engaging with public services, create fear in our workplaces and heighten vulnerability to exploitation. Sajid Javid should concentrate on building a Home Office that people can trust instead of just rebranding the same unfounded hostility.
>
> (Cited in Savage and Cadwalladr, 2019)

So, if Theresa May's 'really hostile environment' is actually intensifying, what then is to be done? The first thing to make clear is that until May goes, nothing is likely to change. As Jamie Grierson (2018) points out, there is a belief within the Home Office that as long as May is Prime Minister, there will be no dramatic departure from the status quo, with one former official stating with respect to her obsessions with reducing immigration and retaining the 'really hostile environment':

> She's very wedded to this tens of thousands target. She's wedded to the hostile environment albeit with a different name. It's going to be difficult for any home secretary to put their own stamp on things.
>
> (Cited in Grierson, 2018)

From a socialist perspective, there are two interrelated steps to be taken. First, the urgent prerequisite is to get rid of the Conservative Government; second and concurrently, there is a need to promote longer-term socialist ideas, including public pedagogy not just for the end of the hostile environment, not just for the dismantling of neoliberal capitalism, but for the end of capitalism itself. I will deal with each in turn. But first I need to address the current state of world capitalism, under whose hegemony there exists a widely acknowledged crisis in neoliberalism, a crisis that is receptive and potentially conducive to the promotion of public pedagogies for socialism. To understand this crisis, a brief historical detour is necessary.

The crisis in neoliberalism

The central parameters of neoliberal capitalism

The neoliberal consensus dominated global politics for at least two decades, since the advent of its two pioneers in the west, Ronald Reagan in the US and Margaret Thatcher in the UK. Reagan started his presidency in 1981 and Thatcher became leader of the Conservative Party in 1975. Reaganomics meant widespread tax cuts, decreased social spending, increased military spending and the deregulation of domestic markets (Kenton, 2018), while under Thatcher over 50 major companies privatized or sold (Osborne, 2013). In his first year of office, Reagan fired more than 11,000 striking air traffic controllers who ignored his order to return to work (Glass, 2008), while one of Thatcher's biggest neoliberal victories was the smashing of the great miners' strike of 1984–1985. In order to understand how the crisis in neoliberalism came about, it is necessary to identify neoliberalism's central parameters. Bramble (2018) summarizes the main features of the neoliberal project, with respect to its effect on workers and structural changes in the capitalist system:

> In terms of the attack on the working class, they included: mass redundancies, reductions in the minimum wage, repression of the trade unions and imposition of aggressive private sector managerialism

in the public sector to weaken the power of organised labour; remaking the welfare system to focus more on surveillance and control over the working class to make it more susceptible to heightened exploitation by capital; greater emphasis on 'user pays' in the provision of public services, education and healthcare; and, finally, a switch from progressive and direct taxation to regressive and indirect taxation.[1]

Neoliberalism led to:

the steady expansion in the fortunes of the rich, a shift of national income from labour to capital, a rise in corporate profitability and the growth of inequality, reversing the trend towards reduced disparities in income that had marked the period from the end of the Great Depression [of the 1930s] until the 1970s. Trade unions were pulverised, with coverage rates falling to historic lows, and strikes collapsed.

(Bramble, 2018)

In the 1980s and 1990s, democratic input into politics was removed as regressive economic policies were forced through, with politics being reduced to discussions about trivia, since the big decisions had already been made by unelected bodies (Bramble, 2018).

As far as the restructuring of capital is concerned, the neoliberal offensive involved privatising state-owned industries; reducing tariffs and quotas (government taxes on imports and quantity limits respectively) to allow more efficient businesses to benefit more from international trade and investment; a high interest rate regime to squeeze inflation and force out marginal businesses; widespread use of outsourcing (handing over control of public services to private enterprises); and deregulation (removing or reducing state control) of the financial sector. The overall aim was to switch capital out of sectors where its return to the capitalist class was marginal or negative towards those where the capitalist class as a whole could make a higher return (Maisuria and Cole, 2017). 'By the late 1990s', Bramble (2018) concludes, 'the rhetoric of globalisation – a free market trading order with minimal regulation of capital – emerged and added to the neoliberal mix' (Bramble, 2018). In the language of Marxist economics, the major effect of the neoliberal revolution was to reverse the decades-long decline in the rate of profit by raising the rate of exploitation[2] and rationalising constant capital[3] (Bramble, 2018; see also Harman, 2009; Roberts, 2016).

The realization that neoliberalism is not working

There is a broad agreement that we are witnessing a crisis in neoliberalism. In 2018, Marxist scholar and long-time political activist, Tom Bramble wrote:

> That neoliberalism in the West is in crisis is widely accepted across the political spectrum and is a topic that features regularly in the leading international press and in discussions at the highest levels of the ruling class and their advisers at forums and institutions such as Davos, the IMF, OECD, World Bank and the World Economic Forum (see, for example, Wolf, 2018).
>
> (Bramble, 2018)

Whereas the ruling class refer to a crisis in the 'liberal international order' (e.g. Wolf, 2018), for Marxists (e.g. Davidson, 2013; Plavšić, 2017; Bramble, 2018) the crisis in neoliberalism is a crisis in neoliberal capitalism. As Bramble (2018) puts it, the 'crisis has multiple elements, political, economic, social and imperial, which arise out of the organic workings of the capitalist system'. The various elements, he goes on, 'are not superimposed on the system from outside but are the contemporary forms that capitalist crisis in the West takes in the early twenty-first century', a particular feature being the nexus between its economic and political facets. The crisis, he continues, is indicated by two major developments: popular discontent with the austerity and inequality that neoliberalism has produced; and a growing realization by the ruling class that neoliberalism is not working for capitalists as it should be. This crisis in neoliberalism in the West was exacerbated in 2016 by what Joseph Choonara (2016) describes as two further 'wounding blows' to the global neoliberal order: Trump's election and the Brexit vote. Both were also expressions of growing racism in both countries.

Public pedagogy for a borderless socialist future

The urgent need for a Labour Government

Along with despair (Trump in the White House and the processing of Brexit dominated by the hard and far right) the crisis in neoliberalism has also brought hope, as people actively seek alternatives. Thus, for the first time in decades socialism has been projected to the mainstream. Echoing the Italian Marxist theoretician and political leader, Antonio Gramsci, Ben Tarnoff (2018) notes that it is 'easy to feed the pessimism of the intellect, but it's important to find sources of hope to keep fuelling the optimism of the will'. After reflecting on the dire state of affairs globally – burning world, rising water, broken politics, and the state of working-class life in the UK – falling life expectancy and the devastating impact of austerity, Ben Tarnoff (2018) celebrates the 'bright spot in our mostly bleak moment: a rising wave of militancy and mobilisation on the left, particularly the socialist left' in a country 'where the left in general and socialism in particular have been in retreat since the late 1970s'.

'Socialists are no longer constantly losing', he notes. Indeed, they are running for office and engaging in direct action. 'Against the nihilism of the right and the timidity of the centre', he argues, 'they are advancing a vision of a habitable future, one where the working class in all of its variety – young, migrant, queer – can live' (Tarnoff, 2018). Referring to Jeremy Corbyn and Bernie Sanders, Tarnoff (2018) argues that:

> the best basis for optimism might ultimately be the strangeness of the situation we find ourselves in – a situation strange enough to make two old socialists central players in British and US politics. There are junctures in history when the elements come unstuck and rearrange themselves into new and surprising patterns. The course of events becomes impossible to predict. Time moves raggedly, in leaps and ruptures. Another world becomes possible, although there are no guarantees.

The Labour Party's membership has soared with some 350,000 new members (a nearly threefold increase and over half a million total membership as of February 2019), and in the 2017 General Election it saw the largest increase in its vote since 1945, on its most radical manifesto in decades (Labour Party, 2017). Based on an edited collection by John McDonnell (2018), Tarnoff (2018) ascertains the desired outcome of a Britain under Labour:

> a high-wage, high-productivity economy oriented away from finance and towards productive sectors. It's one in which public banks, public investment and public ownership play a significant role, along with a large network of co-operatives. An active industrial policy shepherds the transition to a post-carbon society through a 'Green New Deal', while increased spending on healthcare, childcare and education sustains a robust system of social provision.
>
> (Tarnoff, 2018)

Tarnoff (2018) acknowledges that the Labour programme is, of course, still capitalist: the 'basis of a new social-democratic settlement that pulls

British society in a more humane and egalitarian direction'. He also recognizes that it is 'also an arrangement that capital will fight tooth and nail to prevent'. As I write this (April 2019), a number of accusations of 'Marxist' are being directed at Jeremy Corbyn from Conservatives.

For socialists, in the UK at the present conjuncture there is an urgent need and a real possibility of replacing the Tory Government of Theresa May, or whoever replaces her (possible at any time, given the unprecedented fragility of her government and the bungling of Brexit) with a Labour Government led by Corbyn. Indeed, I would argue that socialists have a political duty to vote for such a government at the next General Election (also possible at any time for the same reasons) as the only way to secure a non-Tory government or Tory-led coalition.

A Labour Party Antiracist Manifesto

A comprehensive antiracist policy for the Labour Party is a priority, particularly given the ongoing multiple manifestations of the 'hostile environment'. The policy should be underpinned by awareness of the historical and enduring multicultural nature of British society, dating back centuries, along with the influence and positive impact this has had on UK society. These could be key elements and considerations of such a policy:

- The 'hostile environment' should be abandoned and replaced by an agenda of social justice and the humane treatment of immigrants, refugees and asylum seekers. Serious consideration should be given to the 'inevitability of a borderless world' (*BBC News*, 2016).
- All forms of racism need to be challenged irrespective of the ethnicity of the perpetrator. To recap, racism encompasses: (1) older colour-coded racism such as anti-black, anti-Asian and anti-Chinese racism (anti-BME racism); (2) older non-colour-coded racism such as antisemitism, anti-Gypsy Roma and Traveller racism, and anti-Irish racism; (3) newer non-colour-coded racism such as xeno-racism directed at eastern Europeans; (4) newer hybridist racism such as Islamophobia and anti-refugee and anti-asylum seeker racism.
- Given the level and degree of accusations of antisemitism in the Labour Party (e.g. *BBC News*, 2019), acknowledged by John McDonnell to be 'a real problem' (*Sky News*, 2019b), the Party might consider a separate Manifesto on Antisemitism.[4]
- Terminology and nomenclature are important: (1) 'Race' is a social construct not a biological given (see Note 5 in Introduction to this book); (2) 'Political Correctness' should be replaced with respect for persons. 'Political correctness' or 'PC' is a pernicious concept

invented by the Radical Right, which, unfortunately, has become common currency. The term was coined to imply that there exist (Left) political demagogues who seek to impose their views on equality issues, in particular appropriate terminology, on the majority. In reality, nomenclature changes over time by those who are included in specific nomenclatures. Using current and acceptable nomenclature is about fostering a caring and inclusive society, not about 'political correctness'; (3) We should use antisemitism spelled this way. The conventional usage has a hyphen between 'anti' and 'Semitism' and a capital 'S' – 'anti-Semitism'. I have omitted the hyphen and used a lower case 's' on the grounds that Jewish communal organizations in the UK – such as the Jewish Socialist Group – use the unhyphenated 'antisemitism'. This more closely reflects Wilhelm Marr's use of the word (Marr popularized the term that he and others advocate to describe a policy towards Jews based on 'racism' (Langmuir, 1990, p. 311, cited in Iganski and Kosmin, 2003, pp. 6–7). Not using a hyphen or a capital 'S' denotes that antisemitism is a form of racism directed at Jewish people per se, and not at those who speak a Semitic language per se. Semitic languages are spoken by nearly 500 million people across large parts of the Middle East, North Africa and Northeast Africa. The most widely spoken Semitic language is Arabic; (4) You do not need to be *a racist* to be racist and one can be racist towards one or more constituencies and not others.

• It should be recognized that these forms of racism can intersect with each other and with other identities: e.g. an elderly black Jewish disabled working class transgender woman faces manifold and multiple oppressions.

The Labour Party and immigration

The election of a Labour Government would not end borders. However, Shadow Home Secretary, Diane Abbott confirmed that Labour would scrap the 'bogus' net migration target, abolish the 2014 Immigration Act and end the 'hostile environment'. In addition 'anyone with specified bona fide skills can come here to work' (cited in *BBC News*, 2018b). Specifically, ending the class-based immigration of the Theresa May Government, a 'new, integrated work visa', 'available to all those we need to come here, whether it is doctors, or scientists, or care workers' would 'offer rights of work and residency and accelerated citizenship to a range of professions, workers and those creating employment who want to come here' (Abbott, cited in *BBC News*, 2018b). This would apply for people coming to take up specific job offers, where it can be shown that those jobs cannot be filled by workers already resident here, with migrants outside the EU being treated with the same fairness as EU migrants after Brexit (Abbott, cited in *BBC News*, 2018b). Yarl's Wood and Brook House (for men at Gatwick Airport) detention centres would be closed (Abbott, cited in *BBC News*, 2018c).

Abbott also vowed to scrap the minimum income requirement for non-EU migrants and to give people 'more rights of family reunion', but Labour would act against illegal immigration and 'make the system of deportation of overseas criminals much easier and smoother' (cited in *BBC News*, 2018b).

The case for a socialist future without borders

John McDonnell has argued, correctly in my view, that '[t]he movement of peoples across the globe will mean that borders are almost going to become irrelevant by the end of this century', that existing borders were being ignored, and that a borderless world is inevitable (cited in *BBC News*, 2016).

Immigrant rights activist and author Teresa Hayter (2004, 152) has elaborated on the ways in which borders are being ignored and the reasons why they do not work. Using the water metaphors commonly applied to immigration, but in terms of controls, she notes: 'controls are like a dam; when one hole is blocked, another one appears somewhere else' (2004, 152). As we have seen in this book, with respect to the attempts to enter the UK via Calais, as well as the attempts to cross the English Channel, migrants display 'staggering feats of ingenuity, courage and endurance to assert their right to move and to flee' (2004, 152). As we have also seen in this book, it is not always easy to deport people, and people spend years in detention. Moreover, deportation is often prevented by legal means, or by public pedagogies, involving anti-deportation publicity and protest.

McDonnell argues that we should thus be preparing for open borders, and also explaining why people move: poverty, conflict and climate change: 'We should be opening up the debate of how we handle [mass migration]' (cited in *BBC News*, 2016). Gary Younge has articulated a public pedagogy of why people move:

> Britain and other western nations actively and intentionally under-developed during colonialism. There we have a historical responsibility. Much of the migration in the world at present, it should be pointed out, is not voluntary but forced, by extreme poverty, natural disasters and wars.
>
> (Younge, 2018)

He has also suggested how we should handle it:

> It would be a better world if people only moved if they wanted to and if they did not have to move to eat. Environmental policies, particularly on climate change, arms controls and responsible foreign and trade policies, would assist in allowing many people to stay where they would rather be – at home. Put another way, those who insist that we cannot afford to take in the world's misery should make more of a concerted effort to ensure that we are not helping to create the world's misery.
>
> (Younge, 2018)

For over a century socialists have engaged in public pedagogy for open borders. Thus in August 1907, the International Socialist Congress, the seventh of the Second International, in Stuttgart, rejected all border controls as follows: 'any economic or political exclusionary rules … are fruitless and reactionary by nature'. 'This is particularly true', it went on (in discourse typical of times when 'race' was considered a scientific given – see Note 5 in Introduction to this book), 'of a restriction on the movement and the exclusion of foreign nationalities or races' (*Weekly Worker*, 2014). It demanded:

> Abolition of all restrictions which prevent certain nationalities or races from staying in a country or which exclude them from the social, political and economic rights of the natives or impede them in exercising those rights. Extensive measures to facilitate naturalisation.
>
> (Cited in *Weekly Worker*, 2014)

Open borders are not, of course, something that are going to happen tomorrow, and there are plenty of politicians and academics who spend large parts of their time *pontificating their views* on media outlets that specialize in public pedagogy, such as BBC television's *Question Time* or BBC radio's *Today Programme*. As Younge (2018) puts it, there you will find 'people going around in circles about what is practical rather than bothering themselves with what is ethical or moral'. 'It's not naïve', he concludes, 'to hope that what does not seem possible in the foreseeable future is nonetheless necessary and worth fighting for':

> we should all be able to roam the planet and live, love and create where we wish … [in] a world with open borders [that] would demand a radical transformation of much of what we have now. It would demand a rethinking not only of immigration, but our policies on trade

and war, the environment, health and welfare, which would in turn necessitate a re-evaluation of our history, of our understanding of ourselves as a species.

(Younge, 2018)

Notes

1 Space does not permit a discussion of the origins of neoliberal capitalism. However, that is provided by Bramble in his article (Bramble, 2018; see also Maisuria and Cole, 2017; Maisuria, 2018.

2 I explained the Marxist theory of the tendency of the rate of profit to fall as capitalism advances in Cole (2019, 113) as follows:

> The central contradiction in the development of capital is 'the project of expelling labour power from the capitalist labour process through technological innovation' (Rikowski, in Rikowski and Ocampo Gonzalez, 2018, 14). The ever-increasing technological drive for productivity, in order to undercut rivals by making commodities more cheaply, means more machines ('dead labour' – since labour produces them) and less labour power (the source of profit) [for a brief explanation, of why labour power is the source of profit – the Labour Theory of Value – see Note 6, in Chapter 1 of this book]. Thus there is a tendency for the rate of profit (the ratio of profit to investment) to fall, meaning that booms get shorter and slumps, longer and longer and deeper and deeper. As Samir Hinks (2012) explains, profit can only come from human labour. '[A]s more and more capitalists invest in the new machinery the average labour time required to produce each commodity falls. This is what makes the rate of profit fall, as the ratio of surplus value to investment falls across the whole system.' It is important to stress that this is only a *tendency* rather than a law. The solution for the capitalist is to attack workers' conditions, for example, by increasing hours without increasing pay, giving workers less breaks, keeping them under greater surveillance and by laying off workers on contracts and replacing them with workers on zero hours contracts at very low rates of pay or the legal minimum wage if there is one.

3 As Bramble (2018) explains, the neoliberal project coincided with the advent of two other factors that further boosted corporate profitability. First, in the 1980s and 1990s, the large-scale implementation of computers and information technology cheapened constant capital (the value of goods and materials required to produce a commodity, as opposed to variable capital, the wages paid to produce it) and allowed a widespread restructuring of industry by making possible much tighter control over business operations extended over larger areas (and thus for example, the introduction of 'just in time' methods and the construction of international supply lines). Second, the arrival of China as a major player in world trade in the 1990s and 2000s was a boon for Western capitalism, in cheapening the cost of imported goods, depressing the value of labour power, and, for some capitalists, providing a big new market for manufactured goods, financial services and resources. For an excellent Marxist analysis of industrial revolutions, culminating in the fourth, and the need for a socialist revolution, see Craven (2017).

4 While quite rightly completely rejecting the absurd notion that the Labour Party, of which I am a member, is institutionally antisemitic, McDonnell has nevertheless acknowledged that the Party must be quicker and sometimes 'more ruthless' in eradicating antisemitism from its ranks (*Sky News*, 2019b). For a spirited defence of Jeremy Corbyn's leadership from over 200 Jewish members and supporters of the Labour Party, see *Guardian Letters* (2019), where the signatories state that Corbyn's 'lifetime record of campaigning for equality and human rights, including consistent support for initiatives against antisemitism, is formidable. His involvement strengthens this struggle.'

Conclusion

This book has been about the escalation of racism in British society, under the guise of a 'really hostile environment for illegal immigrants', following the financial crisis of 2007–2008 and the ensuing Great Recession. This upsurge needs to be viewed in the context of the subsequent ideological choice made by the political supporters of the ruling class to bail out the bankers and to impose austerity measures on the working class. In the first chapter, I began by addressing this economic and political backdrop to the hostile environment. Then, in order to make sense of the relationship between austerity and the hostile environment, forged in a blanket public pedagogy of hate centred on the issue of immigration, I introduced the Marxist concept of racialization. I then looked at the deployment by the Tories of 'the "race" card' in the lead-up to the 2010 General Election that resulted in the ConDem coalition Government. Having set this toxic background, I moved on to an analysis of the first year of this government, during which immigration legislation became a key policy, austerity was unleashed and May made her first major speech on immigration, launched an offensive against the 'immigrant family' and named, created and consolidated the hostile environment itself. This entailed the fostering of a most reactionary climate of fear directed at some of the UK's most vulnerable people, way beyond those classified as 'illegal', who found themselves on the receiving end of racialization, in the form of xeno-racism, as in the case of Eastern European migrant workers, and hybridist racism directed at asylum seekers. The hostile environment was accompanied by draconian policies, regulations, legislation and rules and actions centred on May's ideological and political obsession with reducing net annual migration to below one-hundred-thousand. I concluded the chapter with an analysis of racism in the run-up to the 2015 General Election.

In Chapter 2, I analysed Theresa May's 2015 speech to the Conservative Party Conference, in essence a bid for Conservative Party leadership. In the speech, May continued to use public pedagogies of hate and threat in an attempt to win over the Tory faithful, and to scupper UKIP. I went on to address the 2016 Immigration Act that amounted to a 'doubling up' on 'hostile environment' policies. Following the pro-Europe Prime Minister Cameron's resignation in the light of a 'leave' victory in the EU referendum, May's ambition came to fruition and she became Prime Minister. I then considered her fragile and unstable premiership, under which the 'really hostile environment' continued with a vengeance as May undermined the rights of international students to attend universities. Having called a snap General Election in a bid to crush all opposition to her, she ended up having to do a deal with the right-wing Democratic Unionist Party in a hung parliament. May carried on regardless, accusing EU nationals of 'jumping the queue' to get into the UK and presiding over the 2018 White Paper on immigration, perhaps the biggest single attack on migrant rights in a generation.

In Chapter 3, I began with some general snapshots of the 'really hostile environment' in action in health and education. I went on to consider how hybridist racism impacted on asylum seekers with respect to inferior accommodation, the right to work, detention, and the harrowing nature of being a torture survivor in the hostile environment. I moved on to a consideration of the plight of migrants attempting to cross the English Channel. Next, I looked at access to healthcare for asylum seekers, before showing how the hostile environment had gender implications and specifically impacted on women, with respect to both detention and domestic violence. I concluded the chapter with a critical analysis of the Domestic Violence and Abuse Bill.

In Chapter 4, I first focused on an extraordinary event that became known as the Windrush scandal and that came to light in 2018. British subjects, mainly from the Caribbean, who had arrived in the UK before 1973, having experienced decades of colour-coded racism, were then detained, denied legal rights, threatened with deportation, with some actually wrongly deported as a direct result of the implementation of the 'really hostile environment'. I then considered families more generally who were or are divided, also directly on account of the effects of the hostile environment, as part of Theresa May's assault on family life. In so doing, I illustrated how that environment has extended its tentacles beyond those obviously negatively racialized. In order to underline the class-based as well as racist nature of May's offensive, I concluded the chapter with an examination of what it actually costs in financial terms to obtain various UK visas, and ultimately for those who want it, UK citizenship. At the end of the chapter, I outlined my and my family's personal encounter with the hostile environment, our experiences of being in a divided family, and estimated the costs for us, both financially and emotionally.

In the last chapter of the book, I began by posing the question, is the hostile environment intentional? I then considered whether it is crumbling or being ramped up or both. I moved on to a discussion of what many see as a crisis on neoliberalism, a crisis that is receptive and potentially conducive to the promotion of public pedagogies for socialism. Accordingly, I then made the case for what I consider to be the urgent need for a left-led Labour Government. In so doing, I outlined what such a government might look like before concluding by briefly making the case for a socialist future without borders. I concluded the chapter with Gary Younge's (2018) insistence that we need to re-evaluate our history and our understanding of our 'species being' (Marx, 1844). Such a radical re-evaluation might naturally gravitate towards socialism. Alongside open borders for people, equal rights for immigrants and no racism, here are some prerequisites for a socialist future:

- the redistribution of wealth in as equal a manner as possible
- the democratization of the economy, so that it is owned, and controlled *democratically* in the true sense of the word (rule of the people), *by* and *for* workers and communities
- the production of goods and services for *need* and not for profit
- the basic necessities (free food, drink, housing, healthcare, education, and childcare for all) as a right
- full equality for all, regardless of gender, ethnicity, sexuality, disability and age, irrespective of faith or no faith, and no discrimination on grounds of these identities or any other identity
- no death penalty
- no imperialism, colonialism or militarism
- self-determination for Indigenous Peoples
- the need to address climate change seriously, end fracking, pipelines, and extractivism
- follow the lead of Indigenous Peoples in protecting water, land and air.
   (Adapted from Cole, 2019, 110–111)

It cannot be stressed enough that the last two bullet points self-evidently are a *pre-condition* for the building of socialism. In October 2018, a landmark report by the UN Intergovernmental Panel on Climate Change (IPCC) warned there are only a dozen years for global warming to be kept to a maximum of 1.5C, beyond which even half a degree will significantly worsen the risks of drought, floods, extreme heat and poverty for hundreds of millions of people (Watts, 2018).

At the same time, the devastating onslaughts of neoliberal capitalism are increasingly being questioned, with austerity being exposed as an ideologically driven fraud. Time is running out for humankind to save the planet. It may be the last chance for those of us who refuse to acquiesce in the environmentally destructive hegemonic world capitalist order to engage in revolutionary dialogue.

References

Agerholm, Harriet. 2018. 'Windrush generation: Home Office "set them up to fail", say MPs', *Independent*, 3 July. Available at: www.independent.co.uk/news/uk/home-news/windrush-home-office-set-them-up-fail-mps-affairs-select-committee-a8428041.html

Allegretti, Aubrey. 2018. 'Windrush scandal: Theresa May accused of running "institutionally racist" government', *Sky News*, 22 April. Available at: https://news.sky.com/story/windrush-scandal-theresa-may-accused-of-running-institutionally-racist-government-11342346

Althusser, Louis. 1971. 'Ideology and ideological state apparatuses', in *Lenin and Philosophy and Other Essays*, London: New Left Books. Available at: www.marx2mao.com/Other/LPOE70NB.html

Amnesty International. 2019. 'UK: domestic abuse bill risks failing migrant women'. Available at: www.amnesty.org.uk/press-releases/uk-domestic-abuse-bill-risks-failing-migrant-women

Ashcroft, Michael. 2016. 'How the United Kingdom voted on Thursday … and why', Lord Ashcroft Polls, 24 June. Available at: https://lordashcroftpolls.com/2016/06/how-the-united-kingdom-voted-and-why/

Ashe, Stephen D. and McGeever, Brendan F. 2011. 'Marxism, racism and the construction of "race" as a social and political relation: an interview with Professor Robert Miles', *Ethnic and Racial Studies*, 34 (12).

Asthana, Anushka, Mason, Rowena and Elgot, Jessica. 2017. 'Theresa May calls for UK general election on 8 June', *Guardian*, 18 April. Available at: www.theguardian.com/politics/2017/apr/18/theresa-may-uk-general-election-8-june

BBC Election. 2010. 'National results after 650 of 650'. Available at: http://news.bbc.co.uk/1/shared/election2010/results/

BBC News. 2009. 'European Election 2009: UK results', 8 June. Available at: http://news.bbc.co.uk/1/shared/bsp/hi/elections/euro/09/html/ukregion_999999.stm

BBC News. 2013a. 'David Cameron promises in/out referendum on EU', 23 January. Available at: www.bbc.co.uk/news/uk-politics-21148282

BBC News. 2013b. 'Farage attacks "nasty" immigration posters', 25 Juy. Available at: www.bbc.co.uk/news/uk-politics-23450438

BBC News. 2014. 'Lenny Henry racism row candidate quits UKIP', 29 April. Available at: www.bbc.co.uk/news/uk-politics-27202753

BBC News. 2016. 'Borderless world inevitable, says Labour's John McDonnell'. Available at: www.bbc.co.uk/news/uk-politics-35455023

BBC News. 2017. '"Deport first, appeal later" policy ruled unlawful', 14 June. Available at: www.bbc.co.uk/news/uk-40272323

BBC News. 2018a. 'Brexit: backlash over May's EU nationals "queue jumping" vow', 20 November. Available at: www.bbc.co.uk/news/uk-politics-46274118

BBC News. 2018b. 'Diane Abbott unveils Labour's new immigration policy', 13 September. Available at: www.bbc.co.uk/news/uk-politics-45510623

BBC News. 2018c. 'Diane Abbott: Labour would close two immigration detention centres'. Available at: www.bbc.co.uk/news/uk-politics-44137353

BBC News. 2019. 'A guide to Labour Party anti-Semitism claims', 18 February. Available at: www.bbc.co.uk/news/amp/uk-politics-45030552

BBC Newsnight on YouTube. 2019. 'Theresa May wanted to tighten every single screw she could find on the immigration system', 28 February. Available at: https://twitter.com/BBCNewsnight/status/1101254587309121537

Bogdanor, Vernon. 2012. 'For UK politics the eurozone crisis will bring the deluge', *Guardian*, 28 June.

Booth, Robert and Butler, Patrick. 2018. 'UK austerity has inflicted "great misery" on citizens, UN says', *Guardian*, 16 November. Available at: www.theguardian.com/society/2018/nov/16/uk-austerity-has-inflicted-great-misery-on-citizens-un-says

Bowcott, Owen. 2018. 'Home Office scraps scheme that used NHS data to track migrants', *Guardian*, 12 November. Available at: www.theguardian.com/society/2018/nov/12/home-office-scraps-scheme-that-used-nhs-data-to-track-migrants

Boyle, Danny, Wilkinson, Michael, Dominiczak, Peter, Swinford, Steven, Riley-Smith, Ben and Chan, Szu Ping. 2016. 'Conservative leadership election: Theresa May wins more than half of MPs' votes as Stephen Crabb pulls out and Liam Fox is eliminated', *Telegraph*, 5 July. Available at: www.telegraph.co.uk/news/2016/07/05/boris-johnson-backs-andrea-leadsom-tory-mps-vote-leadership-race/

Bozic, Martha, Barr, Caelainn and McIntyre, Niamh. 2018. 'Revealed: immigration rules in UK more than double in length', (with additional reporting by Poppy Noor). Available at: www.theguardian.com/uk-news/2018/aug/27/revealed-immigration-rules-have-more-than-doubled-in-length-since-2010?CMP=Share_iOSApp_Other

Bramble, Tom. 2018. 'The crisis in neoliberalism and its ramifications', *Marxist Left Review*, 16 (Winter). Available at: http://marxistleftreview.org/index.php/no-16-summer-2018/162-the-crisis-in-neoliberalism-and-its-ramifications#_edn22

British Expats. Ongoing. Available at: https://britishexpats.com/forum/citizenship-passports-spouse-family-visas-uk-196/merged-spouse-visa-issues-sheffield-spouse-visa-chat-thread-899315/

Bulman, May. 2018. 'Yarl's Wood: inside the crisis-hit immigration detention centre', *Independent*, 28 February. Available at: www.independent.co.uk/news/uk/home-news/yarls-wood-inside-experience-hunger-strike-immigration-detention-scandal-a8230056.html

Butler, Dawn. 2018. 'From the Home Office to No. 10, Theresa May has entrenched racial inequality', *Guardian*, 1 May. Available at: www.theguardian. com/commentisfree/2018/may/01/windrush-injustice-minorities-basic-tory-instinct-may-hostile-environment

Butler, Patrick. 2019. Available at: www.theguardian.com/society/2019/jan/28/ deprived-northern-regions-worst-hit-by-uk-austerity-study-finds?CMP=Share_ iOSApp_Other

Campbell, Scott. 2017. 'Real reason why Donald Trump and Theresa May held hands is revealed: US president "is frightened of STAIRS"', *Daily Mirror*, 29 January. Available at: www.mirror.co.uk/news/world-news/real-reason-donald-trump-theresa-9716450

Casalicchio, Emilio. 2017. Available at: www.civilserviceworld.com/articles/news/ vince-cable-theresa-may-suppressed-nine-reports-showing-immigration-benefits

Centre for Cities. 2019. 'Cities Outlook 2019'. Available at: www.centreforcities. org/

Chakrabortty, Aditya. 2018. 'Immigration has been good for Britain. It's time to bust the myths', *Guardian*. 17 May. Available at: www.theguardian.com/ commentisfree/2018/may/17/immigration-good-for-britain-bust-myths-austerity

Children's Commissioner. 2015. 'Skype families', 9 September. Available at: www.childrenscommissioner.gov.uk/2015/09/09/skype-families/

Choonara, Joseph. 2016. 'Is this the end of the neoliberal consensus?' *Socialist Review*, December (419). Available at: http://socialistreview.org.uk/419/end-neoliberal-consensus

CNN. 2019. 'Economic control recognized as domestic abuse in new UK draft law: offenders may face lie-detector tests'. Available at: https://edition.cnn. com/2019/01/21/health/uk-domestic-abuse-bill-gbr-scli-intl/index.html

Cole, Mike. 1993. '"Black and Ethnic Minority" or "Asian, Black and Other Minority Ethnic": a further note on nomenclature', *Sociology*, 27 (4) November.

Cole, Mike. 2011. *Racism and Education in the UK and the US: Towards a Socialist Alternative*, New York and London: Palgrave Macmillan.

Cole, Mike. 2012. 'Introduction: human rights, equality and education', in Mike Cole (ed.) *Education, Equality and Human Rights*, 3rd edition, London: Routledge.

Cole, Mike. 2016. *Racism*, London: Pluto Press.

Cole, Mike. 2018a. 'Racism in the UK: continuity and change', in Mike Cole (ed.) *Education, Equality and Human Rights*, 4th edition, London: Routledge.

Cole, Mike. 2018b. 'Racism and education: from Empire to May', in Mike Cole (ed.) *Education, Equality and Human Rights*, 4th edition, London: Routledge.

Cole, Mike. 2018c. 'Social class, Marxism and socialism', in Mike Cole (ed.) *Education, Equality and Human Rights*, 4th edition, London: Routledge.

Cole, Mike. 2019. *Trump, the Alt-Right and Public Pedagogies of Hate and for Fascism: What Is To Be Done?* London and New York: Routledge.

Cole, Mike. Forthcoming. 'Racism and fascism in the era of Donald J. Trump and the Alt-Right: critical race theory and socialism as oppositional forces', in Vernon L. Farmer (ed.) *Critical Race Theory in the Academy*, Charlotte, NC: Information Age Publishing.

Cole, Mike and Maisuria, Alpesh. 2014. '"Shut the F*** up", "You have no rights here": critical race theory and racialisation in post 7/7 Racist Britain', *Journal for Critical Education Policy Studies*, 5 (1).

Colson, Thomas and Bienkov, Adam. 2018. 'Theresa May told officials to "toughen up" controversial "go home" immigration vans', *Business Insider*, 20 April. Available at: www.businessinsider.com/theresa-may-nick-timothy-home-office-go-home-vans-windrush-2018-4?r=US&IR=T

Coombs, Caroline. 2019. 'Putting a price on love: the minimum income rule for spouse visas', freemovement, 14 February. Available at: www.freemovement.org.uk/putting-a-price-on-love-the-minimum-income-rule-for-spouse-visas/

Cowburn, Ashburn. 2017. 'Election 2017: Theresa May's immigration policy in "chaos" following confusion over timetable for target reductions', *Independent*, 2 June. Available at: www.independent.co.uk/news/uk/politics/election-2017-theresa-may-immigration-policy-timetable-targets-conservative-manifesto-prime-minister-a7768371.html

Craven, Patrick. 2017. Available at: www.dailymaverick.co.za/opinionista/2017-01-05-the-fourth-industrial-revolution-or-socialist-revolution/

Darder, Antonia and Torres, Rodolfo. D. 2004. *After Race: Racism after Multiculturalism*, New York: New York University Press.

Davidson, Neil 2013, 'The neoliberal era in Britain: historical developments and current perspectives', *International Socialism*, 139 (Summer).

Dearden, Lizzie. 2015. 'Tory conference 2015: Theresa May says she will overhaul asylum seeker process – as it happened', *Independent*, 6 October. Available at: www.independent.co.uk/news/uk/politics/tory-conference-2015-theresa-may-to-tell-conservative-party-mass-immigration-is-bad-for-britain-live-a6681231.html

de Noronha, Luke. 2019. 'Sajid Javid's deportation flight shows the hostile environment in action', *Guardian*, 6 February. Available at: www.theguardian.com/commentisfree/2019/feb/06/sajid-javid-windrush-deportation-criminal-jamaica

Dentith, Audrey M. and Brady, Jeanne F. 1998. 'Girls on the strip: constructing a critical feminist pedagogy of difference in Las Vegas, NV'. Paper presented at the AERA: Research on Women and Education SIG Conference, East Lansing, MI, October.

Dentith, Audrey M. and Brady, Jeanne F. 1999. 'Theories of public pedagogies as possibilities for ethical action and community resistance: a curricular notion'. Paper presented at the AERA: Research on Women and Education SIG Conference, Hempstead, NY, October.

Devlin, Ciaran, Bolt, Olivia, Patel, Dhiren, Harding, David and Hussain, Ishtiaq. 2014. *Innovation and Skills Impacts of Migration on UK Native Employment: An Analytical Review of the Evidence*, London: Home Office. Available at: https://assets.publishing.service.gov.uk/government/uploads/system/uploads/attachment_data/file/287287/occ109.pdf

Dodd, Vikram. 2019. 'Met police "disproportionately" use stop and search powers on black people', *Guardian*, 26 January. Available at: www.theguardian.com/law/2019/jan/26/met-police-disproportionately-use-stop-and-search-powers-on-black-people

Dorling, Danny. 2016. 'Brexit: the decision of a divided country', *British Medical Journal (BMJ)*, 354:i3697, 6 July. Available at: www.bmj.com/content/354/bmj. i3697

Doward, Jamie. 2018. 'Families torn apart as visa misery hits foreign spouses', *Guardian*, 18 August. Available at: https://amp.theguardian.com/uk-news/2018/aug/18/visa-britons-foreign-spouses-families-split-hostile-environment

Early Day Motion. 2018. 'INDEPENDENT REVIEW OF HOME OFFICE IMMIGRATION POLICY AND PRACTICE EDM #1182 Tabled 19 April 2018 2017–19 Session. Available at: https://edm.parliament.uk/early-day-motion/51653/independent-review-of-home-office-immigration-policy-and-practice

EIN (Electronic Immigration Network). 2014a. 'Movement Against Xenophobia meeting: Immigration Act codifies racism into British law and will become untenable'. Available at: www.ein.org.uk/news/movement-against-xenophobia-meeting-immigration-act-codifies-racism-british-law-and-will-become

EIN. 2014b. 'Yvette Cooper says Labour would scrap net migration target, Miliband forgets section of speech on immigration', 24 September. Available at: www.ein.org.uk/news/yvette-cooper-says-labour-would-scrap-net-migration-target-miliband-forgets-section-speech-immi

EIN. 2019. 'UN Special Rapporteurs criticise use of terrorism-related legislation to prosecute Stansted 15 anti-deportation protestors', 7 February. Available at: www.ein.org.uk/news/un-special-rapporteurs-criticise-use-terrorism-related-legislation-prosecute-stansted-15-anti

Elgot, Jessica and Walker, Peter. 2019. 'Javid under fire over "illegal" cross-Channel asylum seekers claim', *Guardian*. 2 January. Available at: www.theguardian.com/politics/2019/jan/02/people-crossing-channel-not-genuine-asylum-seekers-javid

Engels, Friedrich. 1884. *Origin of the Family, Private Property, and the State.* Available at: www.marxists.org/archive/marx/works/download/pdf/origin_family.pdf

Equality and Human Rights Commission (EHRC). 2018. 'Asylum seekers in Britain unable to access healthcare', 29 November. Available at: www.equality-humanrights.com/en/our-work/news/asylum-seekers-britain-unable-access-healthcare

Eror, Aleks. 2018. 'Why Britain's Conservatives cannot shake the "Nasty Party" label', *World Politics Review*, 12 June. Available at: www.worldpoliticsreview.com/amp/articles/24867/why-britain-s-conservatives-cannot-shake-the-nasty-party-label

Fekete, Liz. 2001. 'The emergence of xeno-racism', *Institute of Race Relations*, 28 September. Available at: www.irr.org.uk/news/the-emergence-of-xeno-racism/

Forster, Katie. 2017. 'Budget 2017: Philip Hammond accused of back-door NHS privatisation by funding "shady" reform plans', *Independent*, 8 March. Available at: www.independent.co.uk/news/uk/politics/nhs-budget-2017-nhs-privatisation-stps-philip-hammond-back-door-unite-sustainability-transformation-a7619456.html

Free Movement. 2018. 'The immigration white paper is a charter for the wealthy', 21 December. Available at: www.freemovement.org.uk/immigration-white-paper-wealthy-migrants/

Freedland, Jonathan. 2014. 'Scrapping Human Rights Law is an act of displaced fury', *Guardian*, 3 October. Available at: www.theguardian.com/commentis free/2014/oct/03/scrapping-human-rights-law-european-court-ukip

Fryer, Peter. 1984. *Staying Power: The History of Black People in Britain*, London: Pluto Press.

Gayle, Damien. 2019. 'Stansted 15: no jail for activists convicted of terror-related offences', *Guardian*, 6 February. Available at: www.theguardian.com/ global/2019/feb/06/stansted-15-rights-campaigners-urge-judge-to-show-leniency

Gentleman, Amelia. 2017a. '"I can't eat or sleep": the woman threatened with deport-ation after 50 years in Britain', *Guardian*, 28 November. Available at: www. theguardian.com/uk-news/2017/nov/28/i-cant-eat-or-sleep-the-grandmother-threatened-with-deportation-after-50-years-in-britain

Gentleman, Amelia. 2017b. '"They don't tell you why": threatened with removal after 52 years in the UK', *Guardian*, 1 December. Available at: www.theguardian. com/uk-news/2017/dec/01/man-detained-threatened-with-removal-after-52-years-in-the-uk

Gentleman, Amelia. 2019. 'MPs condemn Home Office over new Windrush fail-ings', *Guardian*, 6 March. Available at: www.theguardian.com/uk-news/2019/ mar/06/home-office-woefully-complacent-despite-windrush-scandal-reveals-mps-public-accounts-committee-report?CMP=Share_iOSApp_Other

Giroux, Henry A. 1998. 'Public pedagogy and rodent politics: cultural studies and the challenge of Disney', *Arizona Journal of Hispanic Cultural Studies*, 2.

Giroux, Henry A. 2000. 'Public pedagogy as cultural politics: Stuart Hall and the "crisis" of culture', *Cultural Studies*, 14, 341–360.

Giroux, Henry A. 2004. 'Cultural studies, public pedagogy, and the responsibility of intellectuals', *Communication and Critical/Cultural Studies*, 1 (1).

Giroux, Henry A. 2010. *Hearts of Darkness: Torturing Children in the War on Terror*, London: Paradigm Publishers.

Glass, Andrew. 2017. 'Reagan fires 11,000 striking air traffic controllers, Aug. 5, 1981', *Politico* 5 August. Available at: www.politico.com/story/2017/08/05/ reagan-fires-11-000-striking-air-traffic-controllers-aug-5-1981-241252

Global Justice Now. 2018. 'Campaigners call immigration white paper "biggest attack on rights in Britain in a generation"', 19 December. Available at: www. globaljustice.org.uk/news/2018/dec/19/campaigners-call-immigration-white-paper-biggest-attack-rights-britain-generation

Godwin, Richard. 2018. 'Sajid Javid's cynical headline-grabbing epitomises yet another year of anti-immigrant hysteria', *Independent*, 30 December. Available at: www.independent.co.uk/voices/home-office-sajid-javid-migrants-refugees-kent-beach-donald-trump-caravan-a8704521.html

GOV.UK. 2010. 'Immigration: Home Secretary's speech of 5 November 2010'. Available at: www.gov.uk/government/speeches/immigration-home-secretarys-speech-of-5-november-2010

GOV.UK. 2013. 'Speech by Home Secretary on second reading of Immigration Bill'. Available at: www.gov.uk/government/speeches/speech-by-home-secretary-on-second-reading-of-immigration-bill

GOV.UK. 2016. 'Statement from the new Prime Minister Theresa May'. Available at: www.gov.uk/government/speeches/statement-from-the-new-prime-minister-theresa-may

GOV.UK. 2018. 'Detentions under the Mental Health Act'. Available at: www.ethnicity-facts-figures.service.gov.uk/health/access-to-treatment/detentions-under-the-mental-health-act/latest

GOV.UK. 2019. 'UK visas and registering with the police'. Available at: www.gov.uk/register-with-the-police/who-needs-to-register

GOV.UK. Ongoing. 'Immigration Rules: updates'. Available at: www.gov.uk/guidance/immigration-rules/updates

Grice, Andrew. 2009. 'Review of the year 2009: expenses scandal', *Independent*, 23 December. Available at: www.independent.co.uk/voices/commentators/andrew-grice/review-of-the-year-2009-expenses-scandal-1847865.html

Grice, Andrew. 2015. 'David Cameron rules out third term as PM and reveals favourites for next Tory leader', *Independent*, 23 March. Available at: www.independent.co.uk/news/uk/politics/david-cameron-admits-he-wont-serve-beyond-2020-10128858.html

Grierson, Jamie. 2018. 'Hostile environment: anatomy of a policy disaster'. Available at: https://amp.theguardian.com/uk-news/2018/aug/27/hostile-environment-anatomy-of-a-policy-disaster

Guardian Letters. 2019. 'Jeremy Corbyn's Labour is a crucial ally in the fight against antisemitism'. Available at: www.theguardian.com/politics/2019/feb/20/jeremy-corbyn-labour-party-crucial-ally-in-fight-against-antisemitism

Hansard. 1974. 'Spouses of United Kingdom Citizens (Equal Treatment) Bill', 21 June. Available at: https://api.parliament.uk/historic-hansard/commons/1974/jun/21/spouses-of-united-kingdom-citizens-equal#column_929

Hansard. 2018. Available at: https://hansard.parliament.uk/lords/2018-06-14/debates/4EB5AD24-87B4-43E9-908F-1DE447952889/ImmigrationHostile Environment

Harman, Chris. 2009. *Zombie Capitalism: Global Crisis and the Relevance of Marx*, London: Bookmarks.

Harvey, David. 2015. 'Capital's nature – a response to Andrew Kliman', The New Left Project, 30 March.

Hattenstone, Simon. 2018. 'Why was the scheme behind May's "Go Home" vans called Operation Vaken?' *Guardian*, 26 April. Available at: www.theguardian.com/commentisfree/2018/apr/26/theresa-may-go-home-vans-operation-vaken-ukip

Hayter, Teresa. 2004. *Open Borders: The Case Against Immigration Controls*, 2nd edition, London: Pluto Press.

Hill, Amelia. 2017. '"Hostile environment": the hardline Home Office policy tearing families apart', *Guardian*, 28 November. Available at: www.theguardian.com/uk-news/2017/nov/28/hostile-environment-the-hardline-home-office-policy-tearing-families-apart?CMP=Share_iOSApp_Other

Hill, Dave. 2019. 'Marxist education against capitalism in the neoliberal era', *Cadernos do GPOSSHE On-line* (Grupo de Pesquisa Ontologia do Ser Social, Historia, Educação e Emancipação Humana). Fortaleza, Brazil.

Hinks, Samir Karnik. 2012. 'What is the tendency of the rate of profit to fall?' *Socialist Review*, 371 (July/August). Available at: http://socialistreview.org. uk/371/what-tendencyrate-profit-fall

HM Government. 2019. *Transforming the Response to Domestic Abuse: Consultation Response and Draft Bill, January.* Available at: https://assets.publishing. service.gov.uk/government/uploads/system/uploads/attachment_data/ file/772247/Transforming_the_response_to_domestic_abuse_-_consultation_ response_and_draft_bill_-print.pdf

HM Inspectorate of Prisons. 2017. *Report on an Unannounced Inspection of Yarl's Wood Immigration Removal Centre.* Available at: www.justiceinspectorates.gov. uk/hmiprisons/wp-content/uploads/sites/4/2017/11/Yarls-Wood-Web-2017.pdf

Holton, Kate and Smout, Alistair. 2018. 'May apologises for saying EU workers can't "jump the queue"', *Reuters*. Edited by William Schomberg. Available at: https://uk.reuters.com/article/uk-britain-eu-may-migration-idUKKCN1NV24U

Home Affairs Select Committee. 2018. 'House of Commons Home Affairs Committee The Windrush Generation Sixth Report of Session 2017–19', 27 June. Available at: https://publications.parliament.uk/pa/cm201719/cmselect/cmhaff/ 990/990.pdf

Hughes, Laura. 2017. Available at: www.telegraph.co.uk/news/2017/09/06/pmqs-live-home-office-plans-curb-migration-leaked/

Hunt, Alex. 2014. 'UKIP: the story of the UK Independence Party's rise', *BBC News*, 21 November. Available at: www.bbc.co.uk/news/uk-politics-21614073

Hunt, Alex and Wheeler, Brian. 2017. 'Theresa May: 10 reasons why the PM blew her majority', *BBC News*, 14 June. Available at: www.bbc.co.uk/news/election-2017-40237833

I LOVE MY 'FOREIGN' SPOUSE: defend the rights of cross-border couples. Ongoing. Available at: www.facebook.com/groups/139807999382936/

Iganski, Paul and Kosmin, Barry (eds). 2003. *The New Antisemitism? Debating Judeophobia in the 21st Century*, London: Profile Books.

Immigration Directorate Instructions. 2012. Available at: https://assets.publishing. service.gov.uk/government/uploads/system/uploads/attachment_data/ file/263237/section-FM2.1.pdf

Inman, Phillip. 2019. 'Hammond £5bn short of "austerity is ending" target, says thinktank', *Guardian*, 11 February. Available at: www.theguardian.com/ business/2019/feb/11/hammond-austerity-5bn-short-meeting-target-ifs-promise?CMP=Share_iOSApp_Other

Institute for Economics & Peace. 2018. *Global Peace Index, 2018: Measuring Peace in a Complex World*, Sydney, June. Available at: http://visionofhumanity. org/app/uploads/2018/06/Global-Peace-Index-2018-2.pdf

Jayanetti, Chaminda. 2018. 'NHS denied treatment for migrants who can't afford upfront charges', *Guardian*. Available at: www.theguardian.com/society/2018/ nov/13/nhs-denied-treatment-for-migrants-who-cant-afford-upfront-charges

JCWI (Joint Council for the Welfare of Immigrants). 2016. 'What's next for the Hostile Environment: The Immigration Act 2016 and the Queen's Speech', 23 May. Available at: https://jcwi.org.uk/blog/2016/05/23/what%E2%80%99s-next-hostile-environment-immigration-act-2016-and-queen%E2%80%99s-speech

JCWI. 2018. 'Dossier of Failure'. Available at: www.jcwi.org.uk/dossieroffailure

Kentish, Benjamin. 2018a. 'Theresa May declares "austerity is over" after eight years of cuts and tax increases', *Independent*, 3 October. Available at: www.independent.co.uk/news/uk/politics/theresa-may-austerity-end-over-speech-conservative-conference-tory-labour-a8566526.html

Kentish, Benjamin. 2018b. 'Theresa May accused of fuelling hate crime over claims EU migrants "jump the queue"', *Independent*, 20 November. Available at: www.independent.co.uk/news/uk/politics/theresa-may-eu-migrants-hate-crime-jump-queue-cbi-speech-conservatives-a8643456.html

Kenton, Will. 2018. 'Reagonomics', *Investopedia*, 13 February. Available at: www.investopedia.com/terms/r/reaganomics.asp

Kerr, Donna H. 1999. 'Voicing democracy in an imperfect world: towards a public pedagogy of nurture', in F. Smith and G.D. Fenstermacher (eds) *Leadership for Educational Renewal: Developing a Cadre of Leaders. Agenda for Education in Democracy, Vol. 1*, San Francisco, CA: Jossey-Bass.

Khomami, Nadia and Naujokaityte, Goda. 2018. 'How the Windrush scandal led to fall of Amber Rudd – timeline', *Guardian*, 30 April. Available at: https://amp.theguardian.com/uk-news/2018/apr/30/how-windrush-scandal-fall-amber-rudd-timeline

Kingsley, Patrick. 2012. 'Financial crisis: timeline', *Guardian*, 7 August. Available at: https://amp.theguardian.com/business/2012/aug/07/credit-crunch-boom-bust-timeline

Kirkup, James. 2015. 'Theresa May's immigration speech is dangerous and factually wrong', *Telegraph*, 6 October. Available at: www.telegraph.co.uk/news/uknews/immigration/11913927/Theresa-Mays-immigration-speech-is-dangerous-and-factually-wrong.html

Kirkup, James and Winnett, Robert. 2012. 'Theresa May interview: "We're going to give illegal migrants a really hostile reception"', *Telegraph*, 25 May. Available at: www.telegraph.co.uk/news/uknews/immigration/9291483/Theresa-May-interview-Were-going-to-give-illegal-migrants-a-really-hostile-reception.html

Kliman, Andrew. 2015. 'The Great Recession and Marx's Crisis Theory', *American Journal of Economics and Sociology*, March. Available at: www.researchgate.net/publication/273836047_The_Great_Recession_and_Marx's_Crisis_Theory

Labour Party. 2017. *Our Manifesto*. Available at: https://labour.org.uk/manifesto/

Lambert, Imogen. 2017. 'UK law penalises British citizens for marrying non-Brits', *The New Arab*, 23 May. Available at: www.alaraby.co.uk/english/amp/comment/2017/5/23/uk-law-penalises-british-citizens-for-marrying-non-brits

Langmuir, Gavin I. 1990. *Toward a Definition of Antisemitism*, Berkeley and Los Angeles, CA: University of California Press, with the cooperation of the Center for Medieval and Renaissance Studies, University of California, Los Angeles.

Laws, David. 2010. *22 Days in May: The Birth of the Lib Dem-Conservative Coalition*, London: Biteback.

Lea, Sian. 2016. 'The Immigration Act 2016 in plain English', Human Rights News, Views & Info, 31 May. Available at: https://rightsinfo.org/immigration-act-2016-plain-english/

Lewis, Paul, Barr, Caelainn, Clarke, Seán, Voce, Antonio, Levett, Cath and Gutiér-rez, Pablo. 2019. 'Revealed: the rise and rise of populist rhetoric', *Guardian*, 6 March. Available at: www.theguardian.com/world/ng-interactive/2019/mar/06/revealed-the-rise-and-rise-of-populist-rhetoric?CMP=Share_iOSApp_Other

Lindsay, Caron. 2017. 'In full: Tim Farron's speech: I love my country and I want it back from the nationalists', *Liberal Democratic Voice*, 19 March. Available at: www.libdemvoice.org/in-full-tim-farrons-speech-i-love-my-country-and-i-want-it-back-from-the-nationalists-53681.html

Liverpool Echo. 2013. Available at: www.liverpoolecho.co.uk/news/liverpool-news/birkenhead-mp-frank-field-tells-3320350

Luke, Carmen. 1994. 'Childhood and parenting in popular culture', *Journal of Sociology*, 30, 289–302.

Luke, Carmen (ed.). 1996. *Feminisms and Pedagogies of Everyday Life*, Albany, NY: State University of New York Press.

Lyons, Kate, Thöne, Eva, Kirchgaessner, Stephanie, Baumard, Marilyne and Galarraga, Naiara. 2017. 'Britain is one of worst places in western Europe for asylum seekers', *Guardian*, 1 March. Available at: www.theguardian.com/uk-news/2017/mar/01/britain-one-of-worst-places-western-europe-asylum-seekers

Maisuria, Alpesh. 2006. 'A brief history of British "race" politics and the settle-ment of the Maisuria family', *Forum*, 48 (1), 95–101. Available at: www.wwwords.co.uk/pdf/freetoview.asp?j=forum&vol=48&issue=1&year=2006&article=13_Maisuria_FORUM_48_1_web

Maisuria, Alpesh, 2018. 'Neoliberal development and struggle against it: the importance of social class, mystification and feasibility'. Available at: www.researchgate.net/publication/329226140_Neoliberal_Development_and_Struggle_Against_It_The_Importance_of_Social_Class_Mystification_and_Feasibility

Maisuria, Alpesh and Cole, Mike. 2017. 'The neoliberalization of higher education in England: an alternative is possible', *Policy Futures in Education*, 15 (5).

Margaret Thatcher Foundation. 1978. TV interview for Granada *World in Action* ('rather swamped'). Available at: www.margaretthatcher.org/document/103485

Marx, Karl. 1844. *Economic and Philosophical Manuscripts.*

Marx, Karl. 1870 [1978]. *Ireland and the Irish Question*, Moscow: Progress Pub-lishers.

Marx, Karl. 1887. *Capital, Vol. 1.* Available at: www.marxists.org/archive/marx/works/1867-c1/

Marx, Karl. 1894 [1966]. *Capital, Vol. 3*, Moscow: Progress Publishers.

Mayor of London. 2018. 'Mayor calls to protect victims of serious crime with inse-cure status', 15 August. Available at: www.london.gov.uk/press-releases/mayoral/protect-victims-of-crime-with-insecure-status

McDonnell, John (ed.). 2018. *Economics for the Many*, London: Verso.

McIntyre, Niamh and Taylor, Diane. 2018. 'Britain's immigration detention: how many people are locked up?', *Guardian*, 11 October. Available at: www.theguardian.com/uk-news/2018/oct/11/britains-immigration-detention-how-many-people-are-locked-up

McIntyre, Niamh and Topping, Alexandra. 2018. 'Abuse victims increasingly denied right to stay in UK', *Guardian*, 16 August. Available at: www.theguardian.com/uk-news/2018/aug/16/abuse-victims-increasingly-denied-right-to-stay-in-uk

Mead, Matthew. 2007. 'Empire Windrush: cultural memory and archival disturbance', MoveableType, Vol. 3. Available at: http://discovery.ucl.ac.uk/1572362/1/Matthew%20Mead.pdf

Merrick, Rob. 2019. 'Students wrongly caught up in Theresa May's "hostile environment" still being detained and "living in terror"', *Independent*, 17 February. Available at: www.independent.co.uk/news/uk/politics/students-theresa-may-hostile-environment-immigration-detention-deport-english-tests-a8781731.html

Miles, Robert. 1987. *Capitalism and Unfree Labour: Anomaly or Necessity?* London: Tavistock.

Miles, Robert. 1989. *Racism*, London: Routledge.

Moore, Michael and Ramsay, Gordon. 2017. 'UK media coverage of the 2016 EU Referendum campaign', London: Centre for the Study of Media, Communication and Power The Policy Institute, King's College London, May. Available at: www.kcl.ac.uk/sspp/policy-institute/CMCP/UK-media-coverage-of-the-2016-EU-Referendum-campaign.pdf

Osborne, Alistair. 2013. 'Margaret Thatcher: one policy that led to more than 50 companies being sold or privatised', *Telegraph*, 8 April. Available at: www.telegraph.co.uk/finance/comment/alistair-osborne/9980292/Margaret-Thatcher-one-policy-that-led-to-more-than-50-companies-being-sold-or-privatised.html

Pearce, Tom. 2017. 'UK budget steps up attacks on education', World Socialist Web Site (WSWS), 21 March. Available at: www.wsws.org/en/articles/2017/03/21/educ-m21.html

Penrose, Justin and Wellman, Alex. 2013. 'Donna Oettinger Purley rail deaths: mum had tried to commit suicide just months ago', *Mirror*, 24 March. Available at: www.mirror.co.uk/news/uk-news/donna-oettinger-purley-rail-deaths-1781828

Perkins, Anne and Quinn, Ben. 2018. 'May's immigration policy seen as "almost reminiscent of Nazi Germany"', *Guardian*, 19 April. Available at: www.theguardian.com/uk-news/2018/apr/19/theresa-may-immigration-policy-seen-as-almost-reminiscent-of-nazi-germany

Perraudin, Frances. 2019. 'Home Office criticised for accelerating removals to Zimbabwe', *Guardian*, 12 February. Available at: www.theguardian.com/world/2019/feb/12/home-office-criticised-for-accelerating-removals-to-zimbabwe?CMP=Share_iOSApp_Other

Pimlott, Daniel, Giles, Chris and Harding, Robin. 2010. 'UK unveils dramatic austerity measures', *Financial Times*, 20 October. Available at: www.ft.com/content/53fe06e2-dc98-11df-84f5-00144feabdc0

Plavšić, Dragan. 2017. 'The Tory crisis is the crisis of neoliberalism', Counterfire, 13 June. Available at: www.counterfire.org/articles/opinion/19035-the-tory-crisis-is-the-crisis-of-neoliberalism

PoliticsHome. 2014. 'David Cameron speech to 2014 Conservative Party Conference'. Available at: www.politicshome.com/news/uk/social-affairs/politics/speech/54764/david-cameron-speech-2014-conservative-party-conference

Portes, Jonathan. 2018. 'Austerity really has hit poor people hardest – the figures prove it', *Guardian*, 14 March. Available at: www.theguardian.com/commentis free/2018/mar/14/austerity-poor-disability-george-osborne-tories

Press Association. 2019. 'Javid questions whether cross-Channel migrants are "genuine" asylum seekers', *Isle of Wight County Press*, 2 January. Available at: www.iwcp.co.uk/news/national/17330284.javid-questions-whether-cross-channel-migrants-are-genuine-asylum-seekers/

Prince, Rosa. 2010. 'David Cameron: net immigration will be capped at tens of thousands'. Available at: www.telegraph.co.uk/news/politics/6961675/David-Cameron-net-immigration-will-be-capped-at-tens-of-thousands.html

Reynolds, Sile. 2018. 'This is what the hostile environment did to asylum seekers'. Available at: www.politics.co.uk/comment-analysis/2018/05/08/this-is-what-the-hostile-environment-did-to-asylum-seekers

Richmond Chambers, Immigration Barristers. 2012. 'Summary of key changes to family migration Immigration Rules on 9 July 2012'. Available at: https://immigrationbarrister.co.uk/summary-of-key-changes-to-immigration-rules-on-9-july-2012/

Riddell, Peter. 2010. 'How "inevitable" was the Con-Lib Dem Coalition?', London: Institute for Government, 30 November. Available at: www.institute forgovernment.org.uk/blog/how-inevitable-was-con-lib-dem-coalition

Rikowski, Glenn and Ocampo Gonzalez, Aldo. 2018. 'Interview on Marxism, critical pedagogy and inclusive education: discussions for a revolutionary discourse' (Glenn Rikowski interviewed by Aldo Ocampo Gonzalez), the Center for Latin American Studies on Inclusive Education (CELEI), March. Available at: www.celei.cl/wp-content/uploads/2018/03/Entrevista-sobre-Marximo-Pedagog%C3%ADa-Cr%C3%ADtica-y-Educaci%C3%B3n-Inclusiva_Dr.-Glenn-Rikowski_UK.pdf

Roberts, Michael. 2016. *The Long Depression*, Chicago, IL: Haymarket Books.

Robinson, Nick. 2013. 'Economy: there is no alternative (TINA) is back', *BBC News*, 7 March. Available at: www.bbc.co.uk/news/uk-politics-21703018.

Rose, Steven and Rose, Hilary. 2005. 'Why we should give up on race: as geneti-cists and biologists know, the term no longer has meaning', *Guardian*, 9 April. Available at: www.theguardian.com/world/2005/apr/09/race.science

Russell, Neal. 2018. 'As an NHS doctor, this "hostile environment" has made me reject my medal', *Guardian*, 23 July. Available at: www.theguardian.com/commentisfree/2018/jul/23/nhs-doctor-ebola-medal-migrant-patients

Ryder, Nicholas. 2014. *The Financial Crisis and White Collar Crime: The Perfect Storm?* Cheltenham: Edward Elgar.

Salmon, Rachel. 2014. 'The 2014 Immigration Act 2 June 2014', Rachel Salmon, LGiU Policy Briefing. Available at: www.lgiu.org.uk/wp-content/uploads/2014/06/The-2014-Immigration-Act.pdf

Sandlin, Jennifer A., O'Malley, Michael, P. and Burdick, Jake. 2011. 'Mapping the complexity of public pedagogy scholarship: 1894–2010', *Review of Educational Research*, September.

Sandlin, Jennifer A., Schultz, Brian D. and Burdick, Jake. 2010. *Handbook of Public Pedagogy*, New York: Routledge.

Savage, Michael and Cadwalladr, Carole. 2019. 'Revealed: how Home Office hires out staff to hunt migrants', *Guardian*, 16 February. Available at: www.theguardian. com/uk-news/2019/feb/16/home-office-hires-out-staff-hunt-migrants-hostile-environment?CMP=Share_iOSApp_Other

Sharma, Ruchira. 2018. 'Here's every single public immigration failure under Theresa May since 2016', The i Newsletter, 19 April. Available at: https://inews. co.uk/news/politics/windrush-immigration-theresa-may/amp/

Shattuck, John, Watson, Amanda and McDole, Matthew. 2018. Available at: https:// carrcenter.hks.harvard.edu/files/cchr/files/trumpsfirstyeardiscussionpaper.pdf

Siddique, Haroon. 2019. 'Minority ethnic Britons face "shocking" job discrimination', *Guardian*, 18 January. Available at: www.theguardian.com/world/2019/ jan/17/minority-ethnic-britons-face-shocking-job-discrimination?CMP=Share_ iOSApp_Other

Simon, Roger. 1992. *Teaching Against the Grain: Texts for a Pedagogy of Possibility*, Westport, CT: Bergin and Garvey.

Simon, Roger. 1995. 'Broadening the vision of university-based study of education: the contribution of cultural studies', *The Review of Education/Pedagogy/ Cultural Studies*, 12 (1).

Sky News. 2019a. 'Interview with Clare Moseley', 31 January. Watched live by the author.

Sky News. 2019b. 'John McDonnell: Labour "must be more ruthless" on antisemitism', 3 March. Available at: http://news.sky.com/video/share-11653851

Sparrow, Andrew. 2010. Available at: www.theguardian.com/politics/2010/nov/05/ nigel-farage-elected-ukip-leader

Staton, Bethan. 2019. 'Home Office doubles charge for migrants to use the NHS'. Available at: https://news.sky.com/story/home-office-doubles-charge-for-migrants-to-use-the-nhs-11601734

Stevens, Robert. 2013. 'UK Prime Minister Cameron plays the anti-immigrant card', World Socialist Web Site (WSWS), 29 November. Available at: www. wsws.org/en/articles/2013/11/29/came-n29.html

Stewart, Heather. 2016. Available at: www.theguardian.com/politics/2016/jul/13/ theresa-may-becomes-britains-prime-minister

Stone, Jon. 2016. 'What Theresa May said about immigration in her infamous speech to Tory conference', *Independent*, 25 August. Available at: www. independent.co.uk/news/uk/politics/theresa-may-immigration-policies-speech-conference-2015-tory-conservative-party-views-a7209931.html

Summers, Deborah. 2009. 'David Cameron warns of "new age of austerity"', *Guardian*, 26 April. Available at: www.theguardian.com/politics/2009/apr/26/ david-cameron-conservative-economic-policy1

Swinford, Steven 2015. Available at: www.telegraph.co.uk/news/general-election-2015/11592230/Election-2015-How-David-Camerons-Conservatives-won.html

Tarnoff, Ben. 2018. 'Next left: Corbyn, Sanders and the return of socialism', *Guardian*, 17 December. Available at: https://amp.theguardian.com/books/2018/ dec/17/the-next-left-socialism-in-the-uk-and-the-us

Taylor, Diane. 2018. 'UK removed legal protection for Windrush immigrants in 2014', *Guardian*, 16 April. Available at: www.theguardian.com/uk-news/

2018/apr/16/immigration-law-key-clause-protecting-windrush-immigrants-removed-in-2014

Taylor, Diane and Perraudin, Frances. 2019. 'Couples face "insulting" checks in sham marriage crackdown', *Guardian*, 14 April. Available at: www.theguardian.com/uk-news/2019/apr/14/coupl es-sham-marriage-crackdown-hostile-environment

The Children's Society. 2016. Available at: www.childrenssociety.org.uk/sites/default/files/making-life-impossible.pdf

The Coalition: Our Programme for Government. 2010. Available at: https://assets.publishing.service.gov.uk/government/uploads/system/uploads/attachment_data/file/78977/coalition_programme_for_government.pdf

Thorn, Lyka. 2013. 'Factory life'. Available at: https://rikowski.wordpress.com/2013/12/04/factory-life-by-lyka-thorn/

Tomlinson, Sally. 2019. *Education and Race from Empire to Brexit*, Bristol: Policy Press.

Townsend, Mark. 2018. ' "I left my daughter at nursery. I didn't see her for a month": how UK splits migrant families', *Guardian*, 5 August. Available at: www.theguardian.com/uk-news/2018/aug/05/child-separation-migrant-parents-uk-hostile-environment-trump

Townsend, Mark. 2019. 'Just 6% of vulnerable detainees released from UK immigration centres', *Guardian*, 9 February. Available at: www.theguardian.com/uk-news/2019/feb/09/vulnerable-detainees-released-from-uk-immigration-centres?CMP=Share_iOSApp_Other

Trading Economics. 2019. Available at: https://tradingeconomics.com/united-kingdom/inflation-cpi

Travis, Alan. 2013. 'Tory immigration language "like National Front of 1970s" ', *Guardian*, 25 September. Available at: www.theguardian.com/uk-news/2013/sep/25/tory-immigration-language-national-front-yvette-cooper

Travis, Alan. 2017a. 'May pressured NHS to release data to track immigration offenders', *Guardian*, 1 February. Available at: www.theguardian.com/uk-news/2017/feb/01/home-office-asked-former-nhs-digital-boss-to-share-data-to-trace-immigration-offenders

Travis, Alan. 2017b. 'UK asylum seekers' housing branded "disgraceful" by MPs', *Guardian*, 31 January. Available at: www.theguardian.com/uk-news/2017/jan/31/uk-asylum-seekers-housing-branded-disgraceful-by-mps-yvette-cooper

Trend, David. 1992. *Cultural Pedagogy: Art/Education/Politics*, Westport, CT: Bergin and Garvey.

UK SPOUSE VISA. Ongoing. Available at: www.facebook.com/groups/UK.IMMIGRATION2015/

UN WOMEN. 2016. 'Global database on violence against women'. Available at: http://evaw-global-database.unwomen.org/en/countries/europe/united-kingdom-of-great-britain-and-northern-ireland/2002/domestic-violence-concession-under-the-immigration-rules

Usborne, Simon. 2018. 'How the hostile environment crept into UK schools, hospitals and homes', *Guardian*, 1 August. Available at: www.theguardian.com/uk-news/2018/aug/01/hostile-environment-immigrants-crept-into-schools-hospitals-homes-border-guards

Vassiliou, John. 2019. 'Media pressure saved my clients from removal – but now come the crippling fees', freemovement.org.uk, 25 February. Available at: www.freemovement.org.uk/media-pressure-saved-my-clients-from-removal-but-now-come-the-crippling-fees/

Verma, Rahul. 2018. 'It was standard to see signs saying, "No Blacks, No Dogs, No Irish"', *Human Rights News, Views & Info*, 29 November. Available at: https://rightsinfo.org/racism-1960s-britain/

Virdee, Satnam. 2014. *Racism, Class and the Racialized Outsider*, London: Palgrave.

Virdee, Satnam and McGeever, Brendan. 2017. 'Racism, crisis, Brexit', *Ethnic and Racial Studies*, 41 (10). Available at: www.tandfonline.com/doi/full/10.1080/01419870.2017.1361544

Visram, Rozina. 1986. *Ayahs, Lascars and Princes*, London: Pluto Press.

Walvin, James. 1973. *Black and White: The Negro and English society 1555–1945*, London: Allen Lane.

Watts, Jonathan. 2018. 'We have 12 years to limit climate change catastrophe, warns UN', *Guardian*, 8 October. Available at: www.theguardian.com/environment/2018/oct/08/global-warming-must-not-exceed-15c-warns-landmark-un-report

Waugh, Paul. 2018. 'No Black Caribbean Britons accepted on Civil Service Fast Stream, despite record number of applicants', *HuffPost*, 27 April. Available at: www.huffingtonpost.co.uk/entry/no-black-caribbean-britons-accepted-on-civil-service-fast-stream-despite-record-number-of-applicants-civil-service-fast-stream-dawn-butler-windrush-grandchildren_uk_5ae2ecc7e4b02baed1b922a1?guccounter=1

Weale, Sally. 2018a. Available at: www.theguardian.com/education/2018/may/09/children-denied-free-school-meals-because-of-parents-immigration-status?CMP=share_btn_tw

Weale, Sally. 2018b. 'DfE set to axe pupil data-sharing deal with Home Office', *Guardian*, 9 April. Available at: www.theguardian.com/uk-news/2018/apr/09/dfe-set-to-axe-pupil-data-sharing-deal-with-home-office?CMP=twt_gu

Webber, Esther. 2016. 'Key moments in the EU referendum campaign', *BBC News*, 23 June. Available at: www.bbc.co.uk/news/uk-politics-eu-referendum-36595226

Weekly Worker. 2014. 'Border controls: reactionary by nature', translated by Ben Lewis, 4 April. Available at: http://weeklyworker.co.uk/worker/1004/border-controls-reactionary-by-nature/

White, Michael and Perkins, Ann. 2002. Available at: www.theguardian.com/politics/2002/oct/08/uk.conservatives2002

Whitehead, Tom. 2009. 'European elections 2009: Ukip claims political breakthrough', *Telegraph*, 8 June. Available at: www.telegraph.co.uk/news/worldnews/europe/eu/5478468/European-elections-2009-Ukip-claims-political-breakthrough.html

Whitfield, Kate. 2018. 'Theresa May speech in full: read the PM's punchy Tory conference speech', *Express*, 3 October. Available at: www.express.co.uk/news/politics/1026247/theresa-may-speech-in-full-read-prime-minister-tory-conference-speech/amp

Wilson, Graham, K. 2017. 'Brexit, Trump and the special relationship', *The British Journal of Politics and International Relations*, 19 (3). Available at: http://web.a.ebscohost.com/ehost/pdfviewer/pdfviewer?vid=1&sid=1eb66e62-477f-43b3-a504-cb025cc41dbd%40sessionmgr4006

Wilson, Rob. 2010. *5 Days to Power: The Journey to Coalition Britain*, London: Biteback Publishing.

Wolf, Martin. 2018. 'Davos 2018: the liberal international order is sick', *Financial Times*, 23 January. Available at: www.ft.com/content/c45acec8-fd35-11e7-9b32-d7d59aace167

Womack, Amelia. 2018. 'Theresa May – meet with the Yarl's Wood hunger strikers before it's too late'. Available at: https://inews.co.uk/opinion/comment/yarls-wood-amelia-womack-hunger-strike/

Wright, Oliver. 2016. Available at: www.independent.co.uk/news/uk/politics/david-cameron-resigns-resignation-brexit-eu-referendum-result-live-latest-prime-minister-general-a7099936.html

Wright, Robert. 2018. 'Home Office tells couple it divided to stay together on Skype', *Financial Times*, 15 May. Available at: www.ft.com/content/38dfc2bc-575e-11e8-bdb7-f6677d2e1ce8

www.parliament.uk. 2013. Immigration Bill: 'Written evidence submitted by Rights of Women (IB 11)'. Available at: https://publications.parliament.uk/pa/cm201314/cmpublic/immigration/memo/ib11.htm

www.parliament.uk. 2014. 'The work of the Immigration Directorates (January–June 2014) – Home Affairs Committee: a single immigration target'. Available at: https://publications.parliament.uk/pa/cm201415/cmselect/cmhaff/712/71204.htm

Yarl's Wood Immigration Removal Centre. 2019. Available at: www.yarlswood.co.uk/

Yeo, Colin. 2017. 'The immigration rules for adult dependant relatives: out with the old ...', freemovement.org, 8 November. Available at: www.freemovement.org.uk/out-with-the-old/?utm_source=Free+Movement&utm_campaign=f8b8f99a15-Welcome_series2_3_2016&utm_medium=email&utm_term=0_792133aa40-f8b8f99a15-116351629&mc_cid=f8b8f99a15&mc_eid=89f70db705

Yeo, Colin. 2018. 'Above-inflation increase in immigration and nationality fees for 2018/19', freemovement, 20 September. Available at: www.freemovement.org.uk/increase-immigration-nationality-application-fees-2018-19/?utm_source=Free+Movement&utm_campaign=f8b8f99a15-Welcome_series2_3_2016&utm_medium=email&utm_term=0_792133aa40-f8b8f99a15-116351629&mc_cid=f8b8f99a15&mc_eid=89f70db705

Yeung, Peter. 2016. 'Theresa May "to further scrutinise student visas" in immigration crackdown', *Independent*, 24 July. Available at: www.independent.co.uk/news/uk/politics/theresa-may-immigration-student-visas-brexit-uk-degrees-foreign-students-a7153246.html

Younge, Gary. 2018. 'Dare to dream of a world without borders', red pepper, 30 July. Available at: www.redpepper.org.uk/dare-to-dream-of-a-world-without-borders/

Index